W9-CZU-119

HOW TO HELP YOUR KIDS CHOOSE TO BE TOBACCO-FREE

Other Newmarket Books
by Robert Schwebel

Saying No Is Not Enough: Helping Your Kids Make Wise Decisions about Alcohol, Tobacco, and Other Drugs

Who's on Top, Who's on Bottom: How Couples Can Learn to Share Power

HOW TO HELP YOUR KIDS CHOOSE TO BE TOBACCO-FREE

A Guide for Parents of Children Ages 3 through 19

Robert Schwebel, Ph.D.

Foreword by George D. Comerci, M.D.

Newmarket Press   New York

Copyright © 1999 by Robert Schwebel

This book is published in the United States of America and Canada.

FIRST EDITION

10 9 8 7 6 5 4 3 2 1

Library of Congress Cataloging-in-Publication Data

Schwebel, Robert.
    How to help your kids choose to be tobacco-free : a guide for parents of children ages 3 through 19 / Robert Schwebel ; foreword by George D. Comerci. — 1st ed.
      p. cm.
    Includes index.
    ISBN 1-55704-368-X (hardcover)
    1. Children—Tobacco use—Prevention.   2. Teenagers—Tobacco use—Prevention.   3. Tobacco habit—Prevention.   4. Smoking—Prevention.   5. Parenting.   I. Title.
    HV5745.S38   1999
    649' .4—dc21   99-33797
                                                CIP

QUANTITY PURCHASES

Companies, professional groups, clubs, and other organizations may qualify for special terms when ordering quantities of this title. For information, write Special Sales, Newmarket Press, 18 East 48th Street, New York, NY 10017, call (212) 832-3575, or fax (212) 832-3629.

Text design by Mercedes Everett

Illustrations by Jennifer Harper

Manufactured in the United States of America.

For information regarding speaking engagements by the author, call Dr. Robert Schwebel in Tucson, Arizona, at (520) 748-2122 or write to him care of Newmarket Press at the address above.

This book is dedicated to the memory of my brother, Andrew Schwebel. It is also dedicated to my wife, Claudia; my children, Frank and Henry; my parents, Milton and Bernice; and to all parents who want to raise healthy, wonderful children.

■ Contents ■

Foreword

Responsible parents, for generations, have worried about their children using tobacco. Long before David A. Kessler, M.D., former Commissioner of the U.S. Food and Drug Administration, declared that tobacco addiction is a pediatric disease, parents were aware that the problem almost always begins during the childhood years. A person who hasn't started smoking by age 19 is unlikely to ever become a smoker. Of all current smokers, 80 percent began smoking by the age of 18.

Parents have a powerful influence in the lives of their children, but the job of parenting with regard to the prevention of substance abuse has in the last 30 years become more difficult and much more challenging. Many parents are deeply concerned about protecting their children from drugs but do not know how to do so. This is due in part to the fact that they cannot recall ever having had such discussions with their own parents. In today's world, then, parents need all the information, help, and guidance they can get if they are to be successful in preventing or stopping the use by their children of tobacco and other harmful addictive drugs.

Dr. Schwebel provides important information, helpful insights, and practical suggestions for parents confronted with (1) a young child vulnerable to the impact of advertising and other social pressures to experiment with tobacco, (2) the youngster who has begun to experiment, and (3) the adolescent who has become a regular tobacco user or who may already be physically and psychologically dependent on its use.

In this book, Dr. Schwebel offers parents a better understanding of why in our society children are so attracted to the use of tobacco. He provides an approach that parents can use to counter this attraction. Reading this book will enable parents to learn strategies to help their children understand the harsh realities of tobacco use and to realize the benefits of choosing to be tobacco-free.

GEORGE D. COMERCI, M.D., F.A.A.P.
Former president, American Academy of Pediatrics,
and Professor Emeritus of Pediatrics and Family and
Community Medicine, University of Arizona

HOW TO HELP YOUR KIDS CHOOSE TO BE TOBACCO-FREE

CHAPTER ONE

The Challenge

Raising Tobacco-Free Children

When a local school district asked me to conduct a workshop on tobacco prevention for parents, I had just begun helping Joshua, a nineteen-year-old college student, kick his smoking habit. Bright and articulate, he seemed to be the perfect "volunteer" to help parents get into the mind of a young smoker. I asked if he would participate, and he was happy to do so.

I taped the session, which began with Joshua telling his story: "I smoked my first cigarette when I was thirteen. I was in San Diego on vacation with my parents. I met these other kids at the beach—some of them were older than me—and they had cigarettes. They seemed so cool. I never even thought about smoking before. They offered me a cigarette. I knew it was wrong, but I thought it would be exciting. I was kind of curious. So I smoked a few cigarettes with them and tried not to gag. I hated it and coughed a lot—but it was fun."

Because of the nature of the workshop, it was not surprising that one of the mothers asked: "Didn't your parents talk to you about tobacco? Didn't you know it was dangerous?"

"My parents never really talked with me about tobacco," Joshua said. "But they used to tell me that smoking was dangerous, real dangerous. And I knew it. And they knew that I knew it. But during that first summer I thought that smoking was just a vacation thing, and there was no way I would ever get addicted."

One reason I like telling this particular story is that it shows, as do the statistics from the Surgeon General's Report *Preventing Tobacco Use Among Young People*, that smoking is an issue for all parents. Joshua was part of the 70 percent of children in this country who "try" smoking at least two or more times. Many of these kids wander into it innocently, just as Joshua did. The average age at which children start to smoke is now estimated at between twelve and fourteen.

Joshua explained at the workshop that he didn't smoke again for more than a year. But he was feeling uncomfortable with peers during his first semester as a freshman in high school, and started thinking about smoking as a way to "look cool."

"So at parties," he said, "I started hanging out with smokers and accepting cigarettes when they were offered. I think I was smoking because I felt so awkward. It gave me a way to fit in. Then I started to spend more time with people who smoked and they sort of expected me to smoke, so I kept on doing it. The only cigarettes I bought myself during the first few months was one pack that I smoked alone at home to learn how to inhale. After a while, though, I felt like I had to buy some, too, to be fair."

Indeed we parents should be concerned: in the United States, more than three million adolescents smoke cigarettes today, and more than one million, including almost 20 percent of male high school students, use smokeless (powdered snuff or chewing) tobacco. Another staggering statistic is that three thousand children start smoking every single day. *The Monitoring the Future Project*, an annual survey and report of drug use among American youth conducted at the University of Michigan, found that almost 30 percent of high school seniors become regular smokers.

"Weren't you worried about getting addicted?" a parent asked Joshua.

"I never even thought about it. I thought this was a temporary thing, kind of a 'kid thing,' and that I would do it for a while and then quit. It was cool. It was working for me. It helped me make friends. It took a long time before I realized that cigarettes kind of calmed me down, too. And I liked that. I started smoking more and more and more. But I didn't even notice that I was smoking like, oh, I don't know, more than a pack a day, and I still thought I could stop whenever I wanted, and figured I would stop soon."

"Did your parents find out?" someone asked.

"They didn't find out for a long time. But when they finally did, they hit the roof. They told me they wouldn't allow me to smoke anymore—and grounded me. At first I fought them. But that just made things worse. So then I told them that I'd quit. I never really quit, but I got *real* sneaky. I had been a good kid. My grades were good and I never used to get in trouble. But when they didn't like what I was doing— they just got angry at me, and mean. That made me angry and I guess, mean, too. So part of the fun of smoking was sneaking behind their backs. I feel bad about it now."

Joshua's story shows the importance of being more vigilant about the possibility of our children smoking. It also shows how important it is to respond to the initial use of tobacco in constructive ways that help our children make better health decisions, rather than in aggressive ways that only breed more rebellion.

Joshua was smoking a pack and a half a day when he came to me. He had tried to quit twice before, and failed. But he was highly motivated to change, especially because of a girlfriend who issued an ultimatum, but also because of his concern about the health consequences. He did finally quit, and is currently a nonsmoker, which is another reason why I like to tell Joshua's story: it not only shows that we need to do more with tobacco prevention, but also that there are many ways to help people who are already addicted.

Fighting for Our Children

I wrote this book to support parents who want their children to choose to be tobacco free. It's never too early to start with tobacco prevention. And, it's never too late to help children who are already smoking. Scientists and clinicians have gained a great deal of knowledge about tobacco prevention and cessation. It's a great challenge to raise tobacco-free kids today, but we can protect our children's health.

First and foremost I suggest you start right now. Don't sit on the sidelines and hope for the best. Tobacco should be a child-rearing consideration in every family. Consider this: if your children don't use tobacco products before the age of eighteen, it's unlikely that they will start later. Eighty-nine percent of the adults who smoke on a daily basis started before they turned eighteen. Also, early adolescence is the peak age for first use of smokeless tobacco. But beware: these facts have not escaped the attention of tobacco industry executives who want to convince your children to smoke. For years the tobacco giants aimed their $6-billion-a-year advertising and promotional programs at your kids. So if you want tobacco-free children, you'd better start early and come out fighting.

PARTY ALL NIGHT.
PLAY ALL DAY.

These words are printed in big, bold, red letters against a flashy black-and-gray background on the cover of a magazine insert. Flip to the back page and find some more bold lettering:

RIVER RAFTING
COOKOUTS
FLY FISHING
BONFIRES
MOUNTAIN BIKING
BANDS

In the bottom, right corner is the Marlboro insignia.

Open the insert and you find more bold lettering in white, red, and black.

250 WINNERS.
250 FRIENDS.
PARTY AT THE MARLBORO RANCH.

Now if you were a teen, would this be enticing or what? Even the clever wording of the disclaimer adds to the mystique: "Limited to smokers 21 or older." Read between the lines, and the message is clear: "Smoking is an activity for grown-ups," which, by the way, is quite an appealing pitch to teenagers who may be concerned about their image and would like to appear "grown-up."

Tobacco marketing campaigns, with promotions such as this are already successful—so successful that we're in the midst of a public health crisis. Increasing numbers of youth are using tobacco products, and starting at younger ages. The health consequences are enormous. Of the three thousand Americans under the age of eighteen who begin smoking each day, one of three who continue to smoke in adulthood will die prematurely from smoking-related disease. Tobacco causes more than 400,000 premature deaths each year in this country. Compare this to 100,000 due to alcohol and 20,000 due to *all* the street drugs combined.

Most people are aware of the connection between tobacco use and life-threatening illness. Often overlooked, however, is the equally important fact that *all* tobacco use is harmful, even for those who do not die from it. As physician/author Tom Ferguson wrote in *The No-Nag, No-Guilt, Do-It-Yourself Guide to Quitting Smoking*: "Every cigarette you smoke harms your body." The same can be said about smoking a pipe, every cigar, and every chew of tobacco.

In addition to its inherent risks and harm, tobacco is also a "gateway drug." It serves as an entry point to a lifestyle that could eventually include the use of other drugs with the potential for abuse. This isn't to say that every smoker will eventually graduate to other drugs. However, for those who may be prone to substance abuse, tobacco is a stepping stone toward dealing with life's problems and one's own moods by using chemical substances.

Because the harm and health risks of tobacco are so great, you might think that our task is simple: give children scary information about the dangers of this drug and they will be too frightened to ever use it. Not so. In fact, programs that only give children scary information about drugs actually increase their use, apparently by stimulating curiosity about the "forbidden fruit." More recently, it has been found that teaching about the dangers of tobacco is important, and can be effective in prevention efforts—but only when included as one component in a *comprehensive* program. As you will see, this book offers a comprehensive approach to preventing tobacco addiction, with a special emphasis on helping young people learn to make good decisions, and on preparing them to meet their social and emotional needs *without tobacco*.

The Decision to Use Tobacco

Decision making about health issues is rarely as simple and straightforward as it may appear to be. Many people who know about the dangers of tobacco still choose to smoke or chew it, just as people who know they are taking risks continue to eat high-fat diets, drive without wearing seat belts, or practice unsafe sex.

One reason people use tobacco products is because they are addicted to them. However, before they became addicted, they chose to smoke for other reasons. The bottom line is that people who use tobacco *like* the benefits of this drug—what they are getting or believe they will be getting from it—more than they are concerned about the harm.

The Benefits vs. the Harm

The benefits of using tobacco products vary from person to person and can change over time. Many people start because they are curious and want to know what it feels like. Some young smokers and chewers see tobacco as a way to look or feel "grown-up." Others like the excitement of trying something forbidden or rebelling against their parents. Many people believe that using tobacco products will enhance their image by making them appear "cool," attractive, sexy, or rugged.

As their experimentation with tobacco continues, many smokers discover that they like the effects of the drug: the energy boost, or the fact that cigarettes relax them, or serve to reduce boredom. They may also like the social benefits— fitting in or feeling more comfortable in a tobacco-using crowd. Some smokers like the simple activity of holding a cigarette—it's a social prop. These physical, social, and emotional benefits are what regular smokers most often give as their reasons for using tobacco.

What about the harm? Doesn't the harm outweigh the benefits? These days, most people know that there are significant health risks associated with the use of tobacco, for example, that it is addictive and implicated in many forms of cancer. However, there are also considerable knowledge gaps and misconceptions about other health risks, as well as a variety of psychological defense mechanisms that keep people from gaining full awareness of the potential harm.

One knowledge gap is that some people know that cigarettes cause cancer but don't realize that they are also a contributing cause of heart disease and emphysema. A misconception about tobacco is that smokers only risk getting a disease later in life. Many people don't realize that tobacco is harmful in day-to-day living and leads to more immediate health concerns, such as respiratory infections (bronchitis, laryngitis, and the like) and a weakened respiratory system. Another misconception is that smokeless tobacco—which includes chewing tobacco (wads or plugs of tobacco that are chewed) and pulverized snuff (powdered tobacco put between the gums and cheeks)—is a safe alternative to cigarettes. It is not. Smokeless tobacco is dangerous, putting users at risk for various cancers, heart disease, gum disease, and tooth decay. Although in this book I sometimes use the expression "smoking cigarettes" for simplicity of language when talking about the consumption of tobacco, this reference equally applies to the use of smokeless tobacco. From time to time I will mention smokeless tobacco and use the verb "chewing"—just as a reminder that we are talking about *all* uses of tobacco. They are all harmful.

Another especially important misconception about tobacco occurs when beginning smokers seriously underestimate the risk of addiction. They mistakenly believe that experimenting with tobacco will not significantly increase the risk of becoming a regular smoker. They know tobacco is addictive but think, "I can't get hurt—I'm just dabbling." Eventually many of them are surprised to discover that they are hooked. Researchers found that 73 percent of teenagers who smoked on a daily basis, but predicted they wouldn't be smoking in five years, were still smoking after five years had passed. A recent study found that boys who start smoking as teenagers will end up smoking for an average of 16 years and girls for an average of 20. Some will smoke less than the average, some more than the average, and some for a lifetime.

In addition to knowledge gaps and misconceptions, a variety of psychological mechanisms keep people from feeling the full impact of information about the dangers of tobacco. For example, some people automatically assume, for no good reason, that they are immune to harm—"It won't happen to me." Adolescents are particularly prone to this type of thinking. Also, many adolescents lack a future orientation. This means they are not concerned about health consequences that seem many years away, too remote to matter. Their rationalizing resembles that of people who go into debt by buying on credit. They are more concerned with immediate gratification and pleasure than with what will result later from their behavior.

Uninformed, misinformed, feeling immune to harm, and lacking a future orientation, many smokers claim indifference about the risks. It's easy to say "I don't care" when they lack the ability to project ahead or don't believe that they will be harmed.

Satisfying a Need

Some people who use tobacco are aware of the dangers but continue to do it anyway. They are driven by physical, social, and emotional needs that, in their minds, supersede the harm and risks. For example, some people smoke or chew tobacco because they are tense and uptight. Their emotional need to calm their nervousness outweighs all of their health concerns. Some people smoke or chew to socialize with peers. Their need to conform or "fit in" with a group simply outweighs their concerns about their health.

Making Better Choices

People make decisions about using tobacco by comparing the benefits and harm. *To prevent tobacco addiction, we must help young people understand that the harm outweighs the benefits.* This means breaking through the barriers that prevent them from seeing and fully understanding the harm. It also means doing what we can to decrease the attractiveness of the benefits.

Awareness of the harm can be increased by providing accurate information and by helping people transcend their own defense mechanisms.

There are two very important ways to reduce the perceived benefits of using tobacco. One is by making the use of tobacco products less "cool." In part, this is accomplished by countering and debunking the aggressive advertising of the tobacco industry, which attempts to glamorize the drug and make its use seem attractive and more prevalent than it actually is.

Another way to counter the benefits is to help young people develop other ways to take care of themselves without using tobacco. For example, many of the benefits from tobacco are emotional. Smokers often say:

- "I smoke when I'm tense or anxious. It calms me down."
- "I smoke when I'm angry. It cools me off."
- "I smoke when I'm bored. It's something to do."
- "I smoke when I'm in a tense social situation. It helps me feel comfortable."

To the extent that young people can solve stress-arousing problems or learn healthy ways to cope with stress and unpleasant emotions (for example by deep breathing or engaging in aerobic exercise), they will have less need for tobacco products. Similarly, to the extent they feel comfortable in social situations without tobacco, they will also have less need for the drug. With less need, tobacco itself will be seen as less desirable.

The Stages of Tobacco Use

Research studies have identified five stages of smoking initiation that show how people evolve into addicted smokers. These stages provide valuable clues about how we can intervene to prevent addiction. Not all people move through all five stages. Someone can stop at any point along the continuum. As parents, we want to stop the progression through these stages.

The first or *preparatory stage* is when attitudes and beliefs about what one gets from smoking are formed. During this first stage, children establish a mind-set about tobacco. They may see it as something positive, such as a great way to socialize and have fun, or as something negative, such as a waste of money and a foolish thing to do. Or, they may have a combination of negative and positive attitudes about the use of tobacco. Therefore, the first line of defense against tobacco addiction is raising children who want to be physically healthy, understand the dangers, and have negative attitudes about smoking. Hopefully they will not even experiment with this dangerous drug.

The second or *trying stage* of cigarette use encompasses the first two or three times a person smokes. Many children and adolescents have no interest whatsoever in experimenting with tobacco. Much as we would like *all* of them to stay away from it, the majority of them try smoking. Similarly, large numbers of adolescents try smokeless tobacco. To prevent tobacco addiction, parents must be prepared with effective, age-appropriate responses to children and adolescents who try this drug.

The third stage of tobacco use, known as the *experimental stage*, involves repeated but irregular smoking episodes, generally in response to a situation (such as a party) or to a particular person (such as a best friend).

The fourth stage, *regular use*, is when someone smokes on a regular basis, at least twice a week, and increasingly across a variety of situations and personal interactions.

On average, the span of time between the initial trying stage and the stage of regular use is two to three years, with much individual variation. Two main factors affect the progression in these stages. One is the influence of peers. Smoking often occurs with peers in various social settings. We need to help children learn to resist negative peer influence. The other factor is people discovering that tobacco satisfies their social and emotional needs. These are the benefits of tobacco discussed earlier. To reduce the benefits we must prepare young people to meet their needs without tobacco. Children need to know how to relax and calm themselves down, how to manage their anger, how to have a good time, and how to relate comfortably with peers.

The fifth stage of tobacco use, *nicotine dependence and addiction*, is characterized by a physiological need for nicotine. Addicted smokers need increasing amounts of tobacco to get the effect they seek. For them, it's too late for prevention. Once addicted, smokers may be alarmed about the dangers and want to quit but nevertheless feel that they cannot succeed in quitting. They feel they must have tobacco, and experience withdrawal symptoms when they go without it. At this point, some people rationalize their drug use by saying something like: "You gotta die sometime. Might as well enjoy life." But the truth is that more than 70 percent of addicted smokers would like to quit. Unfortunately, it's easier said than done. That's why *prevention* is of such paramount importance.

Stopping the Progression Toward Addiction

The rest of this book is organized to help you, as parents, prevent your children from moving through the stages I have described. Chapter two is about talking with young children. The emphasis here is on helping them understand the dangers of tobacco and developing negative attitudes about its use. Also discussed is how to set standards and enforce rules about the use of tobacco products; how to respond to violations; and how to react constructively to your children's mistakes, problems, and impulsive behavior. Children often test many aspects of the limits of adult authority, including their parents' stand on the use of tobacco products. You want to maintain your authority, while preserving an open, warm, and safe family climate. You want your children to be able to talk with you about anything.

Although we can stress the danger and harmfulness of tobacco products, eventually most children will become aware of some of the benefits of tobacco—whether from advertising, adults who tell the truth, peers who tempt them, or their own experimentation. Chapter three is about preparing children for this eventuality by teaching them the basic skills necessary to successfully meet their *emotional needs* without tobacco.

Chapter four is about preparing children to meet their *social needs* without tobacco. It has been shown that peer influence often contributes to trying tobacco and to early use. This chapter focuses on a particularly valuable life skill for raising tobacco-free children: the ability to resist negative peer influence. It also discusses how to teach your children to say no; how to encourage them to become leaders rather than followers; how to teach them about good relationships; and how to help them think independently about what is important to them, and what is truly "cool."

Chapter five pertains to talking with older children and teenagers about tobacco. With this age group it's important to have interactive, give-and-take discussions. We want to reduce the numbers of young people who even try smoking. Nevertheless we live in a drug-filled world and must anticipate the strong possibility that adolescents, who are working at defining their independent identity, might experiment with tobacco. This chapter discusses how to open the dialogue and how to respond appropriately to all adolescents, whether or not they have used tobacco.

Chapter six discusses how to counter some of the major roadblocks to clarity that arise in discussions with teens about the costs and benefits of using tobacco. Chapter seven discusses how to make agreements and rules about tobacco. It also includes recommendations about how to increase the motivation for change among teens who are already smoking, but not yet willing to quit.

Sometimes parents are too late for prevention. If a child has already developed a serious tobacco habit, it's important to help him or her quit. Chapter eight is about tobacco cessation.

Good Health Practices—A Long-Term Strategy

It's important to put our effort at preventing tobacco addiction into the context of something bigger—health education. We want to help children learn to love and care for their bodies and minds.

Long before children are tempted to use tobacco products, we begin health education by helping them learn to make good decisions, including good health decisions. This is the foundation on which tobacco prevention—and all drug-abuse prevention—is built. Several aspects of health education merit special attention because they are highly relevant to future behavior with tobacco products.

Consumer Attitudes

This aspect of health education concerns what we put in our bodies and what we don't, especially with regard to food and medicines. Using tobacco or other drugs is an act of consuming. We want children to think carefully about what they consume. Therefore, helping your children learn to value good nutrition and to make wise food choices is vitally important. Your efforts could include lessons about the food pyramid, eating to excess, food additives and chemicals, and the perils of junk food. This may seem obvious, but I was concerned by a recent report that appeared in the *Journal of Pediatrics* stating that only one percent of American young people ages two to nineteen eat healthful diets. I was also concerned by a finding cited in the U.S. Department of Agriculture survey *What We Eat in America* about the dramatic increase in consumption of soda and high-calorie beverages by youth in recent years, and a related statistic that 21 percent of American children ages 12 to 19 are obese. Still another alarming trend is the enormous amount of caffeine consumed by youth in sodas and coffee. High doses typically make children nervous, anxious, fidgety, frustrated, and quicker to anger. Their behavior mimics that of individuals diagnosed with attention deficit hyperactive disorder. Various health risks are also associated with the rising use of caffeine by children. Parents must set an example of good nutrition and recognize that we are in charge of purchasing and preparing food for young children. We set the standards. It is in early childhood that the groundwork is laid for life-long eating habits.

Another aspect of consumerism we want to look at is the manner in which medicines are handled in the family. You can teach your kids prudent attitudes about drugs by demonstrating great care and moderation in the use of medicine. Let your children see you carefully reading the labels and inserts from medicines. Explain that you take only the right amount at the right time and that misuse of medication can mean that the benefits are lost or, worse, that harmful and sometimes dangerous reactions can occur. Additional lessons about medicine include telling children that they should only take medicine when it is given to them by you or another responsible adult. Discussions with children should make it clear that people have to be fully informed in order to decide whether to take medicine, how much to take, and how often. You can also teach about prescription medications—they are taken only under a doctor's supervision and only by the person for whom they are intended. Finally, in your own family, you can demonstrate non-pill solutions to medical problems, such as learning to relax to deal with insomnia or headaches, and using nutritional and herbal remedies for various problems.

Household Substances and Environmental Hazards

Tobacco smoke and tobacco juice from smokeless tobacco are environmental toxins. We want children to think carefully about the harm that comes from polluting their bodies with these substances. We can start by teaching children about poisons and environmental toxins, and how to protect themselves from these substances. Household substances that are dangerous when swallowed should be kept away from food and out of the reach of children, on high shelves or in locked cabinets. Examples of these substances are hair dye, hair spray, nail polish and nail polish remover, drain and oven cleaner, lotions, furniture polish and cleaners, bleach, cosmetics, perfumes, gasoline, weed killer, and insect sprays. Even some indoor plants are toxic. Medicines and vitamins should also be kept out of the reach and sight of children.

Although adults provide protection at first, children eventually need to learn the safety rules regarding household substances. Show them cartons or containers that have labels indicating that the contents are dangerous. Instruct them not to taste, touch, or smell these items.

Exercise and Physical Fitness

Physical fitness is counter to the use of drugs. To raise tobacco-resistant children, make fitness and physical activity a family value. Help your children find vigorous physical outlets for their energy, such as participation on various team sports. You can share many physical activities together, such as swimming, hiking, biking, or tennis. Providing recreational and physical activities is another way of teaching children to care for their bodies.

There is much that can be done. As you continue to read this book, you will discover this inspiring fact: The tobacco industry is no match for parents who raise their children to make wise health decisions and to meet their physical, social, and emotional needs without drugs.

CHAPTER TWO

An Early Start

Talking about Tobacco with Young Children

On a vacation trip during the height of the tourist season, I searched desperately for a room for my family late one night in Saratoga, New York. My sons were three and six years old at the time. After finding many "No Vacancy" signs, I finally discovered space in the Holiday Inn. When we opened the door to the room, we were dismayed by the stench of lingering cigarette smoke. We returned to the front desk and were pleased to find that we could move to a smoke-free room.

The next morning, my wife and I seized the opportunity to start a family discussion about tobacco. We asked our sons what they thought of our smoky room the night before. They said it was awful, and added that smoking is "smelly and dirty." We agreed with them and also talked about the health dangers of tobacco. The discussion lasted for about five minutes. Apparently it made an impression. Nine months later our younger son, who by then had turned four, surprised me when he asked, "Do you remember that stinky room?" It took me a moment to realize that he was referring to our first room in the Holiday Inn.

"Oh yeah," I said. "I remember. Cigarettes smell bad, don't they?"

"Yes," my son agreed, "and they can kill you, too."

Discussions about tobacco should begin when your children are young. Your kids will probably agree with you that using tobacco products is a bad habit. Most young children think that it is undesirable and unattractive, and as they would put it, "gross." They will agree that it is dangerous, too. If you start the discussions early, you will reinforce their negative attitudes about tobacco and build resistance to the forces that glamorize tobacco products.

You don't need a big drumroll to start a discussion. Many opportunities present themselves in everyday life—such as our smelly hotel room—to stimulate a discussion of cigarettes and other tobacco products.

Imagine this: You're in the clean-air section of a restaurant, right next to the smoking area. Two people light up cigarettes at the next table, and smoke drifts in your direction. You and your children are disturbed by the smell. You ask to move to a different table farther away from the smokers. This is an opportunity to talk about tobacco.

Or: You're driving down the road and see someone throwing a cigarette butt out the car window. On the same trip, you see someone spitting tobacco juice on the sidewalk. These, too, are good times to bring the subject up.

Or: A friend is visiting and wants to light a cigarette in your home.

Or: You just saw a movie in which the courageous lead character smoked a lot of cigarettes.

Or: You pass a billboard portraying young, slim, attractive people smoking cigarettes in a beautiful forest setting.

These are natural times to start tobacco discussions— an important part of health education for young children. We know that future smoking and chewing are influenced to a large extent by attitudes and beliefs about tobacco products, and about what they can "do for you," formed during childhood. Bear in mind: people who use tobacco products tend to see them as something that will serve a positive function, such as enhancing their self-image, helping them relax, helping them bond with peers, or providing a way to display independence from parents.

Advertisers recognize the importance of starting early, too. Until recently they used cartoon characters to market their products to young children and awarded prizes, such as gym bags, hats, T-shirts, and other gear, to appeal to teenagers. And in a way it makes sense: They have to recruit young, new smokers to fill the ranks of those who die or quit. Advertisers know that nearly all first use of tobacco occurs before high school graduation and that children are the chief source of new customers. Although the tobacco industry makes more than $270 million annually in profits from selling tobacco to minors, it appears the cash is incidental to their main purpose, which is to recruit new customers.

As parents, you want your children to understand that the use of tobacco products is extremely hazardous to their health. You need to powerfully reinforce an understanding of the dangers and harm from tobacco because you are opposing an industry that spends billions of dollars trying to influence your children to have positive attitudes about it.

For many years, tobacco advertising and promotions included print ads, sponsorship of sports events and public entertainment, outdoor billboards, point-of-purchase displays, and distribution of specialty items that appeal to young people. Recently it was found that half the children who smoke own clothing or gear with cigarette logos, which makes them walking billboards for tobacco. Tobacco promotions have been rampant in auto racing. The tobacco industry has sponsored tennis events and advertised widely in stadiums and arenas.

Advertisers Preying
on Your Kids' Vulnerability

What can tobacco do for you? What can you expect to get from smoking or chewing tobacco? Let's consider the perspective of an adolescent. Adolescents are experiencing an often tumultuous period in life during which they are seeking to establish their own independent identities. They are looking for answers to the questions: Who am I? What is important to me? What do I want to become? As they seek to set their own course, they experience a period of uncertainty, experimentation, and vulnerability. They no longer take for granted everything their parents taught them. Tobacco advertisers have preyed on this vulnerability by portraying positive images of smokers, images that appeal to adolescents struggling to form an identity. Smokers are extremely attractive young men and women having a great time in both outdoor and glamorous settings. Smokers are slender. They are engaged in healthy activities and are independent, which is what adolescents are striving to become. Smokers are adventurous, a characteristic often admired by adolescents.

Advertisers try to capture the imagination of adolescents by showing them a way to improve their self-image. Smoking is presented as self-enhancing: It relaxes people, leads to fun and adventure in life, and makes them attractive—all traits that are important to adolescents who are maturing physically and thinking about romantic and sexual relationships. Smoking, they are led to believe, is an exciting pastime, essential to popularity, and a way to bond with peers.

Reinforcing the messages of the tobacco industry is the consumer- and drug-oriented nature of our society. We are constantly bombarded with messages that there is a drug that can fix almost anything. If you have a headache, use a drug. If your back hurts, use a drug. If you feel anxious, use a drug. If you can't sleep, use a drug. And if drugs don't work, buy something or eat something to feel good. One way or another, there is an easy way to fix what you feel, without dealing with the reality of your situation. This cultural context makes the messages of the tobacco industry even more convincing: Tobacco will make your life better. Light up your cigarette, be gorgeous, and join the happy crowd.

Tobacco advertising is currently a hotly contested political issue, with critics labeling it a threat to public health. Whatever the outcome of the political battles, the impact of advertising will remain with us into the foreseeable future, and the need will be great for parents to respond to it. If all tobacco advertising were to be banned immediately, we still would have to deal with the legacy of past images that have glamorized tobacco and made it seem "cool." We also would have to deal with teens who develop an increased desire to engage in an activity that is "so bad they had to ban it." If advertisers were prohibited from taking direct aim at young people, they would still find subtle ways to communicate to the emotions and vulnerability of this age group. Furthermore, the long history of tobacco advertising has contributed to the glamorization of tobacco in popular culture, as reflected in films with lead actors and actresses lighting up on screen. At this time, smoking or chewing tobacco is seen as an attractive activity by a substantial subset of the adolescent population.

Because of a long history of aggressive advertising by the tobacco industry, and a culture of social approval for the use of tobacco products, parents have to be diligent in maintaining their efforts at countering positive images. You have to fight fire with fire. This chapter is about how to raise tobacco-resistant children who hold negative attitudes about tobacco products. This is vitally important, even though young children are not likely even to be tempted to use tobacco for a number of years.

I recommend taking action on five fronts to raise to-bacco-resistant young children:

1. Debunk tobacco advertising.
2. Counter the problem of a superficial and shallow popular culture that sometimes portrays tobacco as "cool" and attractive.
3. Present the dangers and consequences of tobacco in an age-appropriate manner.
4. Set and enforce rules about not using tobacco products.
5. Establish a family climate in which children can talk with you about anything—without fear.

Fostering negative attitudes about the use of tobacco products poses special problems for parents who themselves use them. This dilemma is discussed below, before moving on to further discussion of the five fronts for tobacco prevention.

What If You Are a Smoker?

Parents who smoke worry that it would be hypocritical to insist that their children refrain from smoking. Although their children may embarrass them by accusing them of hypocrisy, their own discomfort is a secondary issue. They still want and need to promote healthy behavior in their children. That's a primary parenting responsibility, calling for a clear message that tobacco products are unhealthy and children should not use them. Even as a smoker, you can do your best to help your children see the downside of tobacco. Sometimes the influence of your smoking is paradoxical: Children see that you are hooked, hate the odor and your preoccupation with tobacco, and vow that they will never make the same mistake themselves.

If you are addicted to nicotine and regret that you smoke, say this to your children. Let them understand what has happened to you and that you hope to spare them the same fate. Obviously, the best thing for all involved is for you to overcome your own addiction. There are at least four good reasons for you to do this:

1. Being a good role model to your children by showing your commitment to your own health.
2. Eliminating secondhand smoke from your home environment.
3. Improving your health for your own sake.
4. Improving your own health for your children's sake. (You wouldn't be reading this book if you weren't clearly committed to being a good parent. If you stop smoking, you will decrease the likelihood of your own premature death and therefore be available to your children for many more years to come.) Sometimes people cannot make difficult changes for themselves, but can for others. You could channel an urge to care for your children into something that would be positive for yourself.

I don't make this recommendation lightly. Tobacco addiction is the toughest addiction to break. Breaking it could be one of the most difficult challenges you will ever face. Often people try to stop and fail several times before they finally succeed. But many do succeed. Chapter eight provides some advice on quitting tobacco and lists other resources that might be helpful to you. If you do not choose to quit, I would urge you to avoid indulging your tobacco habit in the presence of your children.

Teaching Children
to Be Suspicious of Advertising

An excellent way to counter the aggressive advertising of the tobacco industry is by teaching children to look at the strategies behind the ads. There are several benefits to this. One is that it builds a parent-child alliance to resist and oppose what some young people have called "the trickmasters." Children, and especially adolescents, do not want to be controlled by anyone. When they discover the subtle and manipulative techniques employed by the tobacco industry to control their choices, they resent it. Another benefit is that children learn to analyze advertising. They develop media literacy, which means they gain the ability to see how messages are delivered and what they really represent. This increases their critical thinking skills.

I suggest you begin a campaign of closely examining and analyzing tobacco ads with your children. Make it an occasional evening or weekend conversation. Help your children identify the *sales pitch*—how the advertisers are trying to reel in customers. This can be seen in the images of smokers (slim, attractive, sexy, athletic, rugged, popular individuals) and their lifestyle (full of fun, glamour, exciting activities, parties, and friends). Ask your children what advertisers want them to think their lives will be like if they smoke. You will be exposing the subtle implications of the images presented.

Help your children identify *distortions of the truth* in ads. For example, cigarette smokers are portrayed as having healthy, active lifestyles. Yet precisely the opposite is true. Point out that the negative health consequences of tobacco are ignored, or even denied, by these portrayals. Another distortion in print ads is that cigarettes generally do not emit smoke, and are usually extremely small and inconspicuous, as if they had no impact upon the smoker's lungs. The to-

bacco industry is trying to sell a lifestyle by associating tobacco with good times, popularity, and sex appeal, and by
downplaying that it is a toxic drug, destructive to the body.
It's important that your children recognize that they have
been the targets of advertisers.

Point out to your children what tobacco companies
choose to sponsor, such as sports events and music concerts.
The advertisers want potential customers to associate the
use of tobacco with good times and athletic skills. This is particularly ironic in the case of sports, because smoking is
anathema to physical fitness. Advertisers are not concerned
with the truth.

Art activities can be employed in fighting the tobacco industry. Some families have enjoyed making collages about
tobacco advertising. If you want to try this approach, ask
your children to cut out print ads for tobacco products and
paste them on a sheet of poster board. Together, identify the
sales pitch of each ad and write it next to the clipping. For
example, a sales pitch might be: "You'll look great and have
lots of friends if you smoke this particular brand of cigarette." The poster can be hung on a wall at home.

Another art project that some families have enjoyed is to
design and make anti-smoking commercials on a piece of
poster board. Your child can draw the poster and/or cut pho-
tos from magazines for a collage. Both of these art activities
increase your child's media literacy.

The enormous advertising campaigns of the tobacco industry have fostered the perception that the use of tobacco
products is more widespread than it is, and therefore more
socially accepted. Studies have shown that, on the average,
children and adolescents think that the prevalence of smoking is two or three times higher than the actual rate. Those
with the highest overestimates are more likely to become
smokers than those with the most accurate perceptions. To

them, smoking seems normal: "After all, everyone does it." So young people think they should smoke in order to be part of this large and glamorous crowd. To counteract the distortion about prevalence, we can show young people accurate statistics indicating that smoking is not as widespread as they may think. More than 70 percent of high school seniors are *not* regular smokers.

The value of teaching children to be suspicious of tobacco and other advertising cannot be overstated. Advertisements and promotions appear all around us. We want to raise children who make wise, independent choices, as free as possible from coercion and manipulation.

The Influence of Popular Culture

Popular music, television, and films portray various images of the use of tobacco products, some of which are positive. A recent study from the *American Journal of Public Health* reported that 23 percent of VH1 and more than 25 percent of MTV music videos depict musicians or actors smoking. Unlike advertisements, the music videos are not designed to sell products. However, they certainly influence behavior. It's important to discuss with your children the way tobacco and other products are presented in popular culture.

Discuss situations that seem to glamorize or make tobacco use look "cool." This could lead to a discussion of a variety of topics, such as the way dangers tend to be minimized in popular culture (high-speed car chases, violence without pain, liberal use of tobacco and alcohol), and the very important issue of what makes something "cool." The younger your children are when you begin these discussions, the greater the chance of instilling uplifting values in them. Even if you have disagreements about what makes something "cool," a discussion will at least provoke thinking and dialogue.

Presenting the Dangers
of Tobacco to Five-to-Eight-Year-Olds

Part of a comprehensive program of tobacco prevention includes presenting information about the dangers of tobacco in an age-appropriate manner. One good way to help young children, even as young as five to eight years old, understand the harmful effects of tobacco is to have a series of conversations to introduce the concept of pollution. Ask your children if they have heard of this word and what it means to them. Children will come up with different ideas such as "throwing things on the street," or "garbage that people leave everywhere," or "dirty air," or an "oil spill." Validate their ideas and expand their thinking by explaining that pollution means "to make unclean, impure, or dirty." You can discuss how the world around us (our environment) is being polluted—the rivers, lakes, oceans, and air. In this context you can discuss factory smoke, automobile exhaust, and secondhand smoke (from other people's burning pipes, cigars, and cigarettes). You can find pictures in magazines and newspapers to illustrate pollution, or even make a collage. Sadly, you may be able to find visible signs of pollution in your own neighborhood.

Discuss the pollution of public places—such as airports, hotel rooms, and restaurants—with cigarette smoke. Ask your children how they feel when they are in smoky environments.

Even when discussing the grim reality of pollution, we can help children by expressing a positive outlook about the future, for example, by talking about what people are doing to preserve the environment through recycling and other forms of activism. Explain that smoking used to be permitted in movie theaters, on airplanes, and in many public places. These environments were polluted by tobacco. It was the activism of consumers that changed this. Teaching about activism shows children that they have power over pollution and their own destiny.

In the context of environmental pollution, the next leap is to ask your children how people pollute their own bodies. Some young children might say "by eating too much candy and junk food" and others might mention smoking. Discuss how cigarettes pollute the internal environment of the body. We humans need clean air for our health. Tobacco smoke pollutes the air. It contains 4,000 different compounds, many of which are toxic to the human body.

Show your child the illustration on page 30 called "Body Pollution and Respiration." Explain that our respiratory system allows us to breathe. The lungs and airways carry air into and out of our bodies. When a smoker inhales, smoke travels along the airways to the lungs. The chemicals contained in the smoke irritate the lining of the airways and lungs. This causes swelling and the production of mucus, which pools up in the airways.

Ask your child: "Have you noticed that smokers cough a lot?" Explain that mucus causes the coughing. Tell them the following.

"It gets worse: Bacteria and viruses collect and breed in this mucus, causing lots of infections and a greater chance of getting colds, flu, bronchitis, and other respiratory illnesses.

"And it gets still worse: The buildup of tar on the delicate linings of the lungs and airways is a constant irritant. Smoking can cause cancer."

Tobacco also pollutes by staining teeth and causing a bad smell on a smoker's hair, body, and clothing.

A particularly good demonstration to fortify this lesson on pollution is to have a smoker blow a mouthful of cigarette smoke through a tissue or a clean handkerchief. Point out the color of the tissue. Tell your child that this is what happens to lungs when smoke is inhaled. The amount of tar left on the tissue is about the amount each puff leaves in the

Body Pollution and Respiration

When people smoke, the airways swell. Mucus pools up, and bacteria and viruses breed here, causing infections and illnesses. Tobacco also pollutes by staining teeth and causing a bad smell on a smoker's body and clothing.

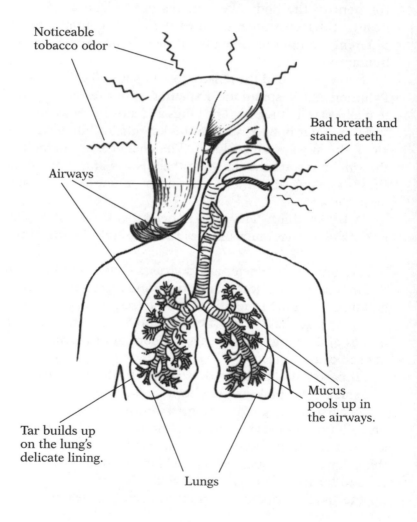

Noticeable tobacco odor

Bad breath and stained teeth

Airways

Mucus pools up in the airways.

Tar builds up on the lung's delicate lining.

Lungs

lungs. This demonstration is so powerful that it has some-times been used to motivate addicted smokers to quit.

Some people think that smokeless tobacco (snuff and chewing tobacco) is a safe alternative to cigarettes because there is no smoke. It is not. A pamphlet from the American Academy of Pediatrics—*Smokeless Tobacco: Guidelines for Teens*—put it this way: "You just move health problems from your lungs to your mouth." Users of smokeless tobacco are at risk for cancer of the mouth (including lips, tongue, and cheek) and throat; leukoplakia (mouth sores); heart disease (because of nicotine in the bloodstream, as with cigarettes); and gum and tooth disease. It can affect one's social life as well: Smokeless tobacco causes really bad breath, discolored teeth, and constant spitting.

Tie together your discussion on health harm and pollution by showing your children the illustration on page 32, which illustrates the effects of tobacco on smokers and chewers. They will see that when people smoke, their sense of smell and taste are impaired; their eyes, nose, and throat are irritated; their lungs receive less oxygen; their heart is forced to pump faster, increasing their blood pressure (which puts them at risk for heart attack and stroke); their fingers and teeth are stained; their blood vessels constrict so their skin is more susceptible to wrinkles; and their blood contains increased amounts of carbon monoxide, which re-places oxygen and causes oxygen deprivation.

A powerful way to reinforce your own efforts in helping children develop tobacco-resistant attitudes is to ask your children's pediatrician and dentist to talk with them about the harmfulness of tobacco. Health care practitioners can begin this practice in a basic way with very young children, and continue the discussion by adding more details through-out childhood.

How Tobacco Affects the Body

The harmful effects of tobacco on the body are numerous.

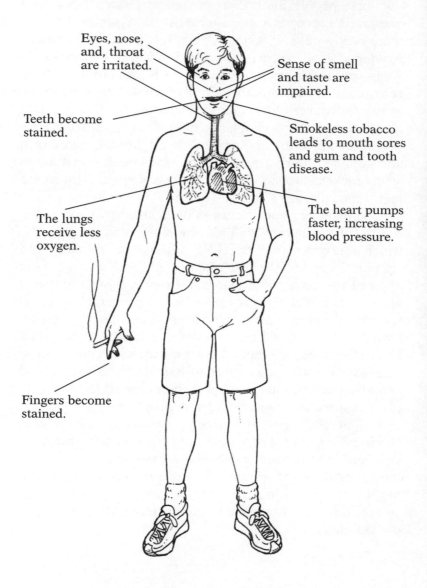

Eyes, nose, and, throat are irritated.

Sense of smell and taste are impaired.

Teeth become stained.

Smokeless tobacco leads to mouth sores and gum and tooth disease.

The lungs receive less oxygen.

The heart pumps faster, increasing blood pressure.

Fingers become stained.

What If Uncle Harry Smokes?

Let's say you have bent over backwards to promote negative attitudes about the use of tobacco in your four-year-old son and six-year-old daughter. You feel that you have been successful but are alarmed when beloved Uncle Harry, a smoker, comes to visit. After the visit you discover your children puffing away at make-believe cigarettes, pretending that they are inhaling.

In situations such as these, I recommend that parents calmly comment on the behavior. A good response could go something like this: "I see you are making believe that you are smoking a cigarette just like Uncle Harry. I know you love Uncle Harry. I love him, too. He's my brother. I hate to see him smoking because it's such an unhealthy habit. I also don't like to see you imitating him because you are copying such a bad habit. I know it's make-believe, but I wish you wouldn't do it." (If the following is true, you can also say: "Uncle Harry has told me that he wishes he could quit. He has tried to stop several times but failed. He feels bad about his habit.")

If the fantasy play persists, you could repeat your concerns later. However, I would not recommend a battle over this type of play because a power struggle could actually increase your children's resistance to your attitude. Generally, "play smoking" gets old and ceases of its own accord if you don't overreact.

Presenting Tobacco Dangers to Nine- and Ten-Year-Olds

With a nine- or ten-year-old you can talk in more detail about addiction. I like to tell kids that addiction actually means being a slave. It is like you have lost a war, and the other side has taken you prisoner. They control you. When you are addicted to a drug, you are controlled by the drug. You need more and more of it. You depend on it to feel okay. You can't live without it. You feel like you can't quit. You spend more and more money getting your drug. You go after the drug even when it is really harming you. You are a slave to it.

Then I let children know that tobacco is one of the toughest addictions to break. Because it is legally available to adults and socially accepted, many young people are very surprised to hear this. They may have heard of cocaine, heroin, or speed and believed that these were tougher addictions, but tobacco is in the same league with them.

Another lesson for this age group concerns the chemicals in cigarettes. In particular you can talk about tars and nicotine. Tars are the main cancer-causing agent in tobacco smoke. They damage lung tissue. Nicotine is a toxin (poison that is harmful and can cause death) that narrows blood vessels, cutting down the flow of blood and oxygen throughout your body. That is why your heart has to pump harder. It raises blood pressure and narrows bronchioles (air passageways) in the lungs, also depriving the body of some oxygen.

At this age children can begin to understand the effects that carbon monoxide—a waste product of cigarette smoke—has on the body. When cigarette smoke is inhaled, this gas replaces oxygen in red blood cells and stays in the bloodstream for hours, depriving one's body of oxygen needed to obtain energy.

Children can also begin to understand some of the diseases caused by the use of tobacco. Cigarettes can cause chronic bronchitis (inflammation of the bronchi, which are the breathing tubes in the lungs), laryngitis (inflammation of the throat), and emphysema (a degenerative lung disease that destroys breathing capacity), and are a contributing factor in cancer of the lungs, mouth, and esophagus. Smokeless tobacco may lead to cancer of the throat and mouth, and to gum disease.

At this age your children can read the Surgeon General's various warnings on tobacco products, which are worthy of discussion. The four warnings rotated on all cigarette packages and ads state the following:

- SURGEON GENERAL'S WARNING: Smoking Causes Lung Cancer, Heart Disease, Emphysema, and May Complicate Pregnancy.
- SURGEON GENERAL'S WARNING: Quitting Smoking Now Greatly Reduces Serious Risks to Your Health.
- SURGEON GENERAL'S WARNING: Smoking by Pregnant Women May Result in Fetal Injury, Premature Birth, and Low Birth Weight.
- SURGEON GENERAL'S WARNING: Cigarette Smoke Contains Carbon Monoxide.

The three warnings rotated on all smokeless tobacco packages and advertising (except billboards) state the following:

- WARNING: This product may cause mouth cancer.
- WARNING: This product may cause gum disease and tooth loss.
- WARNING: This product is not a safe alternative to cigarettes.

Fortifying Negative Attitudes about Tobacco for Nine- and Ten-Year-Olds

A good way to reinforce your efforts in teaching about the dangers of smoking and smokeless tobacco is by calling or visiting the American Heart Association, American Cancer Society, or American Lung Association. Ask for their free literature and read it with your children. Also ask your dentist and family doctor to discuss the dangers of tobacco.

As you focus on the dangers of tobacco, remember that advertisers are promoting their products, and the use of tobacco has gained considerable acceptance among a large subset of youth. Peer influence begins to get important with nine- and ten-year-olds. This is the time to work hard on preparing children to counter the peer pressure to smoke. Chapter four will give you ideas about how to build your child's resistance to negative peer influence.

With children, some of the most dramatic reasons for avoiding tobacco have nothing to do with long-term health consequences. Rather, young people are turned off by the more immediate negative effects of smoking. Tobacco makes your hair and clothing smell bad. It stains your teeth. It makes you unattractive to many of your peers. You can get in trouble for smoking. Also, smoking is an expensive habit. A math exercise can help children get a sense of the enormous expense of a cigarette addiction. With your child, you can go to the store to inquire about the cost of a pack of cigarettes. Then figure out the cost of smoking per day, per week, per month, and per year for someone who is addicted to tobacco and must have a pack a day. Then figure it again for someone who must have two packs a day. With your child, you can finish by playing an imaginary game—thinking of what he or she might buy with the amount of money saved by not smoking a pack of cigarettes per day for a whole year.

Presenting Tobacco Dangers to Eleven- and Twelve-Year-Olds

By the age of eleven or twelve, children are able to understand the concepts of tolerance and withdrawal that underlie addiction and are able to discuss them. These physiological responses to drugs shed some light on how and why people get hooked. For a drug to be physically addictive, it must create both tolerance in a user and a withdrawal syndrome.

Tolerance means that a person needs more and more of a drug to get the same effect. A good way to illustrate this is by referring to a thriller movie that children have seen several times. For example: "Do you remember the thrill you got the first time you saw *Star Wars* (or whatever happens to be the current hot movie)? When you went back the second time, did you get the same thrill? How about the third time?"

"Sometimes drugs are like thriller movies. You want that same feeling, so you keep going back for more. But you're never satisfied the way you were the first time. When this happens with drugs, it's called tolerance. A smoker needs more and more tobacco to feel good when smoking. That's why they may start by only occasionally smoking a single cigarette or two, but eventually find themselves smoking a pack or more every day. They want that same feeling they had at first. But their body has developed a tolerance to nicotine—and they need more of it to get the feeling they want."

As people begin to use more tobacco, they may worry about how much they smoke and feel as though they want to quit. Once they are addicted, however, it's not easy to pull out. When addicted individuals stop using a habit-forming drug, such as tobacco, they will experience a wide range of uncomfortable symptoms during the withdrawal process. Children may have seen documentaries or fictional movies that demonstrate this. They may have seen or heard about "the shakes" that occur when alcoholics quit drinking. You can explain that withdrawal symptoms from tobacco are also severe. They vary from person to person, but typical ones include coughing, sweating, increased sputum production, increased appetite, muscle aches and cramps, nausea, headache, hypersensitivity to physical stimuli, sleep disturbance, and weight gain. Psychologically, some smokers feel foggy-headed, unfocused, and forgetful. They may be irritable, restless, anxious, depressed, and less able to cope with stress. Often people try to quit smoking but feel such discomfort from the withdrawal symptoms that they relapse and resume the old habit.

In addition to understanding tolerance and withdrawal symptoms, older children who have learned about the various diseases associated with tobacco will be ready to learn some relevant statistics. Below are facts about cigarettes and smokeless tobacco that might capture their attention.

In *Smoking: Straight Talk for Teens*, a brochure published by the American Academy of Pediatrics, it is explained that cigarette smokers are more than ten times as likely to die of lung cancer than nonsmokers. Tobacco causes nine out of ten cases of lung cancer and nine out of ten cases of chronic lung disease. It is the main cause of chronic bronchitis, and emphysema, a crippling lung disease. Smoking doubles the chance of heart disease and is one of the three leading causes of heart attacks.

Smokeless tobacco causes cancers of the mouth and throat as well as gum disease.

People who smoke cigars triple their risk of getting lung cancer and double the risk of stroke and heart attack. They increase their risk for cancers of the mouth, larynx, and esophagus. Both pipe and cigar smoking are also risk factors for pancreatic cancer, which is almost always fatal.

Fortifying Negative Attitudes about Tobacco for Eleven- and Twelve-Year-Olds

Persuasive arguments against the use of tobacco products for this age group, as for youth in general, focus on the smell, the cost, and the fact you can get in trouble for smoking or chewing tobacco. Peer influence continues to grow as children near their teens. It is likely that this age group will face an increasing number of opportunities to try tobacco. It is especially important to build "resistance skills," which means the ability to resist peer influence to engage in negative health habits, a topic discussed in detail in chapter four.

Even if accurate information about tobacco prevalence has been given before, this age group should be reminded that more than 70 percent of high school seniors are not regular smokers. Smoking is not such an "in" activity. At this age, children may be interested in learning that most teenagers say they would rather date a nonsmoker. They also should be reminded that no one who tries tobacco expects to get addicted. Most mistakenly believe they will quit in the near future. Once again, pediatricians and dentists should be asked to discuss smoking with your children.

If It's So Bad, Why Do People Smoke?

Bright children of any age who have been warned about the dangers of tobacco will surely wonder, and perhaps ask: "If tobacco is so bad, why do so many people use it?" A good question! I would answer by saying: "Some young people try tobacco because they're curious and encouraged by advertising and promotions that make it seem cool and glamorous. They see peers who've tried it. They don't understand addiction. They think they'll never be harmed and can never get hooked. But some of them discover that tobacco 'works' for them. They like how it changes their mood. They like how it affects their energy level. They like that it makes them feel older. They like that it helps them fit in with a group of smokers. They smoke more and more and are soon surprised to discover they're hooked. None of them thought this would ever happen. They thought it was just a 'kid thing' or a 'teen thing' and that they would stop."

After conceding that some people like the pharmacological effects of tobacco, I would remind children that this drug is a dangerous health risk and that there are many safer ways to feel grown-up, change their moods, and improve their images. I would also say: "As a parent, it is my job to help you learn the good ways to take care of yourself. Then you won't ever *need* tobacco to feel good." Helping children master these life skills will be discussed in chapters three and four.

As a further measure to help put tobacco into perspective, you can have your children interview adult smokers and nonsmokers. Nonsmokers can be asked why they chose to abstain. Smokers can be asked how they started, why they smoke, whether they intended to smoke regularly, if they feel they are addicted, and whether they wished they could quit (remember, more than 70 percent want to quit). Discuss these interviews with your children. In particular, if smokers say they smoke to meet their emotional needs (such as to calm down or relax), you can talk with your children about healthier ways these adults could take care of themselves.

Setting Rules and Having Discussions

It would be a little silly to set a rule against using tobacco for very young children. It would be like saying, "Don't take the family car for a drive" or "You can't go to Paris without my permission." Very young children have no interest in using tobacco products. At about age eight (at the earliest), curiosity might increase about trying tobacco, but children are not likely to seriously pursue the habit. By age eight, you can explain to your children that smoking or chewing tobacco is not permitted.

Firm, nonnegotiable rules will generally prevent young children from using tobacco products. This doesn't mean that a young child may not rebelliously sneak a drag of a cigarette. Your response to such experimentation is important. I like to think of it as parents setting a firm rule, but having a private (unstated) understanding that children are curious and will sometimes test limits. Although we would like to prevent even tobacco experimentation, it could happen. We should be prepared with a constructive response.

I'm certain I shocked my parents when I first experimented with tobacco in the fifth grade. A friend of mine stole cigarettes from his mother, and we went to his "clubhouse," a tiny shack in his backyard. The filter broke off the cigarette I puffed on. (*Puffed* is the word because I didn't know what it meant to inhale.) My friend said that I was going to catch tuberculosis because I smoked a cigarette that had no filter.

"What about nonfilters?" I asked.

"That's different," he answered. "You get tuberculosis from smoking cigarettes when the filters break."

Frightened for my life, I confessed my wrongdoing to my parents that night, hoping I still could be saved. My father reassured me about the particular health concern and then asked what I thought of cigarettes. "Pretty disgusting," I said. He agreed and added that he and my mother did not smoke because "we think they're disgusting, too." He said if I ever wanted more details about why they didn't smoke I could ask. I sincerely said that I was not going to smoke anymore, and that was the end of it.

My parents could have punished me, but I didn't need it. Instead they helped me think through the issue of tobacco in a way I could understand. They showed me that I could talk with them about cigarettes, drugs, or anything without fearing the consequences. Nothing was taboo. The message was: "We're glad you could share the truth with us. Let's talk it over. If you have problems, we can solve them together."

Visionary Parenting

It is relatively easy to control the behavior of young children by simply setting and enforcing rules. However, the problem with relying exclusively on rules is that it does not, by itself, prepare children to think for themselves, nor does it do anything to encourage respectful family discussion. Also, parents need to think ahead and be visionary in child-rearing practices. The strategies for preventing tobacco addiction by adolescents are different from those used with younger children. It is neither helpful, nor appropriate, nor possible, to control the behavior of adolescents. The most powerful way to influence their behavior is by engaging them in dialogue—and the best assurance of a good discussion with an adolescent is a long-standing history of open and clear channels of communication. Too often parents wait for a crisis of some sort—perhaps a drug crisis or some sort of sexual experimentation—before initiating discussion. Instead we should think ahead and start talking during the early years, when children tend to accept parental values. We set precedent by having dialogue, eliciting our children's point of view, listening to their perspective, and allowing for disagreement.

How parents respond to a "hot" subject will set the stage for future dialogue. If a child feels certain topics—such as using tobacco products—are taboo or likely to ignite a firestorm of anger from parents, he or she will never bring them up. We want to make the home environment feel safe for our children to talk with us about anything.

If children do try tobacco, we want them to tell us—just as I told my parents. We want to help them learn to make good choices, not frighten them into silence with harsh and punitive responses. This means establishing a family climate of openness and respect. Such a climate is put to the test when children disagree with us, make mistakes, suffer setbacks, or behave impulsively. In an understanding family, parents recognize that this is part of childhood. We can be a valuable resource for our children by calmly accepting their experiences and giving them a chance to learn from them. This is how we show our love. This is how we help them learn to make wise decisions. So, even as we present the dangers of tobacco and set firm rules, we want to allow for mistakes and maintain an open dialogue with our children.

■ CHAPTER THREE ■

Teaching Children to Manage Emotions without Tobacco

A strong set of anti-tobacco convictions will go a long way toward reducing the odds that your children will experiment with tobacco. But even if you are the greatest parents, and the greatest role models for good health practices, and even if you provide the best discussions about tobacco, you shouldn't be shocked, surprised, or panicked if your children try smoking. Seventy percent of U.S. children do.

There are many reasons your kids may try tobacco. In our drug-crazed society, they're bombarded with pro-tobacco messages that tempt them to smoke. Knowing that we parents oppose their use of tobacco, children sometimes test the limits of our authority. Plus, they're curious and interested in new experiences. Furthermore, one of the developmental tasks of adolescence is to form an independent identity. At this stage in life, they must clarify their own thinking about themselves and their place in the world. To do this, they must explore the world, which could include experimenting with tobacco.

Of the young people who try tobacco, many will cough, gag, hate the taste, and not continue. Others will keep smoking because they are still curious or still motivated by whatever got them to try it in the first place. For those who continue, three factors will profoundly affect their decisions about future use: peer influence, which may or may not provide access to tobacco, and encouragement or incentives for continued use; parental response, which could discourage or inadvertently reinforce continued use; and their own level of personal need for the mood-altering effects of the drug, which I call the drug-neediness quotient (DNQ).

Your Child's DNQ

New smokers quickly discover tobacco's mood-altering effect. If, for example, they feel tense, sad, angry, or bored, they will find that smoking can calm their nerves, lift their mood, cool their anger, or quell their boredom. If they lack adequate, nondrug ways of coping, they will be inclined to use tobacco, or other drugs, to change their mood. In other words, they will have a high DNQ and will be likely to smoke when they feel tense, anxious, angry, or bored. However, if they have adequate non-drug ways of coping, they will have a lower DNQ. They could, for example, solve problems to reduce their stress, resolve relationship conflict to reduce their anger, and structure their lives better so they are not bored. In other words, the DNQ is a measure of how much an individual needs a drug because he or she lacks drug-free ways to successfully cope with daily living. *People with a high DNQ are more likely to feel an urge to continue to use tobacco.*

Think of it this way. If you were often tense and did not know how to relax and then one day discovered the calming effects of cigarettes, you would be strongly attracted to tobacco, especially when you were feeling tense. In the absence of other coping mechanisms, you might come to depend on cigarettes whenever you wanted to relax. You would have a high DNQ.

A high DNQ can override knowledge about the dangers of drugs. In other words, people can be fully informed about the health risks but still choose to smoke or chew tobacco because they have strong personal needs that dominate their decision making.

Drug-neediness can be classified into two categories. One is social drug-neediness—that is, needing tobacco or other drugs in social relationships: to fit in with a peer group, gain popularity, appear "cool" or grown-up, structure time with peers, or feel comfortable in a social setting. Social DNQ is discussed in chapter four. The other category is emotional drug-neediness—that is, needing drugs to cope with negative emotions (such as anger, boredom, sadness, frustration, and anxiety), or to create positive ones. Assessing and reducing your children's emotional DNQ is the topic of this chapter.

When you understand the concept of a DNQ, you can see that a big part of tobacco prevention is not "anti," as in anti-drug or anti-tobacco. Rather it is positive, as in using good childrearing practices to raise healthy, competent children who can satisfy their personal needs without relying on drugs.

Four Goals for Lowering Emotional Drug-Neediness

People who often experience negative emotions and/or have problems coping with these feelings are said to have a high emotional DNQ. They may be tempted to use tobacco to change their moods.

Below I've listed emotional problems in four aspects of living that often trigger tobacco use. After each problem is a corresponding goal that can contribute significantly to lowering emotional drug-neediness. These goals can guide your prevention efforts.

Problem I: Many young people smoke to overcome boredom when they feel there is "nothing to do."

Goal I: You want to make sure that your children know how to have fun and can entertain themselves during leisure time.

Problem II: Many young people smoke because they are tense and want to calm down and relax.
Goal II: You want to make sure that your children can solve problems that could cause stress and can cope successfully with whatever stress is unavoidable.

Problem III: Many young people smoke when they are angry or sad or experience some other unpleasant emotion.
Goal III: You want to make sure that your children are emotionally literate—aware of their own feelings, able to manage their feelings and communicate them effectively, and able to empathize with others.

Problem IV: Many young people smoke to cope with feelings of frustration and failure. Studies have shown that children with lower self-images and lower levels of school achievement are more likely than their peers to use tobacco.
Goal IV: You want to make sure your children have a mastery approach to living. This means that they are experiencing success in school, in family life, in social relationships, and in all important aspects of their lives. When they suffer setbacks or make mistakes, they have the resilience to stay the course and learn from these experiences.

Now let's look more closely at how you can work with your children to achieve these goals. For each goal, I have listed questions to consider when evaluating your children's coping skills. I also have made recommendations about measures that can be taken both to address deficiencies and to help your children maintain success. These recommendations should not only reduce drug neediness but also help your children thrive in general.

Goal I: Fun and Recreation

One of the big motivating factors for using tobacco is boredom. Adolescents say: "I smoke when I'm bored. When there's nothing to do, my friends and I kick back and smoke." You want to make sure that your children know how to have fun and can entertain themselves during leisure time. We need to teach children how to have a good time. It doesn't always come naturally.

The following questions will help you evaluate your children's DNQ in terms of their ability to have fun during recreational time.

Good signs: Do your children have diverse recreational interests? Are they content? Are they fun-loving? Can they create their own excitement?

Bad signs: Do they often complain about being bored? Do they watch a great deal of television? Do they communicate a type of discontent about recreational time, always seeming to crave more excitement?

The following recommendations describe what you can do to reduce your children's drug-neediness quotient with regard to fun and recreation:

1. *Teach your kids that having fun and entertaining oneself are learned skills and a personal responsibility.* Children need to learn to "make fun happen," not to depend on other people, or things they buy or consume, in order to have a good time. Adopt an activist point of view. Explain to your children that boredom is usually within a person, not a situation. Kids say "I'm bored" and have the idea that the world should entertain them. People need to learn to create their own fun and excitement.

When children complain about being bored, I suggest you avoid the habit of telling them what to do. When parents take over, children don't learn how to create their own fun. Instead, teach your children to make recreational decisions.

Help them pay attention to options. For example: "What sort of activity do you feel like doing: an indoor or outdoor one, an active or quiet one, something alone, or with other people?" Then, encourage them to make their own options. "I can't tell you what would be best for you. You have to decide. But you sure have lots of good options." Eventually your children can learn to do this without your assistance.

2. *Discourage television viewing and keep it to a minimum.* Resist the temptation to use television as a baby-sitting device. Children watch far too much television. The average American child watches five to six hours of television per day and will have spent about twice as many hours viewing television as in the classroom by the time he or she graduates from high school. This kind of passive entertainment—sitting and expecting to be amused—is a major reason that so many adolescents get bored and turn to drugs for excitement.

Another problem with television is that the rapidly changing images create restlessness in children. Kids get used to endless novelty and abrupt changes of focus, which together discourage them from developing a long attention span. This bombardment of stimuli has probably had a great influence on the turn toward drugs. A related problem is that television advertising manipulates our kids' consciousness and instills a need to buy, acquire, or consume in order to feel good.

Have your children keep a written record of what they view on television for a week, then discuss it with them—focusing especially on the extent to which the shows and their main characters are positive and uplifting, or violent, scary, and degrading. Count the total hours spent viewing television and, if it is anywhere near half the national average, raise the issue of cutting way back. Try to engage your children in more active and energetic activities instead.

49

Consider the possibility of having a family week, or month, without television, and following this "vacation" with a discussion about how you spent your time.

3. *Help your children appreciate simple pleasures.* Point out beautiful sunsets and picturesque scenery. Listen to the birds with your children. Read to them and teach them the joy of reading. Encourage them to make simple drawings with crayons and to find other types of artistic expression. Listen to music together. Go lightly when it comes to toys—especially with the latest electronic ones that are upstaging and replacing the simpler toys of the past that required an active imagination. To avoid over-stimulation, keep only a limited number of toys on the shelves at once. Help your children enjoy just one toy at a time. They'll soon learn to appreciate the pleasure of quiet and solitary play.

4. *Teach contentment.* In our consumer-oriented society, we are bombarded with messages to buy products and manipulated by the advertising world to consider our lives incomplete and unsatisfactory without them. And so it's not surprising that children often complain that they are unhappy and bored. They're being taught to feel restless, dissatisfied, and discontent unless they buy more goods, so they may start making frequent requests to buy something new. It's as if they believe that they can buy happiness with the purchase of a particular toy or article of clothing, or that they'll be left out if they don't eat at a particular fast-food restaurant. I recommend a firm line on purchases, and resistance to these pressures. When your children aggressively protest that you didn't buy them cotton candy as you leave a playground, en route to a family dinner, resist their pressure. My suggested response is:"We had a good time today. It's important that you learn to be happy with what you have—and we have a lot—instead of going around always wanting more."

Never give in to whining demands for toys. Don't spoil your children by buying them everything they want, even if you can afford it. Such extravagance reinforces the belief that they must always have something new and novel. In my years of working with youth who have tobacco or other substance abuse problems, I have observed this same never-ending quest to feel good, be excited, and be stimulated.

5. *Pay attention to after-school activities.* Think carefully about the after-school hours. This is the time when most juvenile crime occurs. It also could be a time during which homework assignments are completed and special athletic or musical skills are cultivated. The most successful drug prevention programs have been ones that incorporate what is known as "alternative activities," positive recreational outlets that serve as an alternative to drug use and crime. I suggest you assist your children in using after-school time well by providing them with structured activities of some sort in a safe environment with adult supervision. Avoid television and just plain "hanging out."

6. *Develop a "fun list."* An excellent exercise to help children learn to take responsibility for creating their own fun and pleasure is to develop a "fun list." This list becomes a resource your children can refer to when they have spare time. Start by having them list all the things they like to do for fun, and things they think they might like, but haven't yet tried. Remind them of activities you have seen them enjoy.

The important next step is to help expand the list. Think of broadening your children's interests. The idea is not to push them into new activities against their will, but to expand their vision. If their activities tend to be quiet and solitary (computer games), suggest adventuresome ones that might involve friends or family (hiking or camping). Think about calm fun (playing cards) and exciting fun (competitive basketball with an indoor hoop and a nerf ball); indoor activities (playing with Legos) and outdoor activities (picnics); activities that involve creativity (music and art); activities that involve imagination (reading or playing with dolls or action figures); and activities that require discipline (hobbies or mastering a musical instrument). Make sure physical activities are on the list. Encourage your children to think of reading and educational games as fun. Consider after-school activities and various team sports and clubs, such as the Scouts, Boys' and Girls' Clubs, and the 4-H. The fun list can be considered an ongoing work in progress and serve as a reference when children want to have fun or complain about being bored.

If we do not encourage wholesome and broad interests from an early age, then only we are to blame when our children turn to the latest peer fad, electronic gizmo, or high-risk type of excitement for their fun. Family fun not only enhances family pleasure and builds closeness, it also helps children learn the skills of planning for the positive use of leisure time.

Goal II: Managing Stress

Kids say they smoke because they are "stressed out." Many say, "I smoke to relax" or "I smoke when I'm tense." You want to make sure that your children can solve problems that could cause stress and can cope successfully with whatever stress is unavoidable. You can help your children learn to plan their lives to prevent unnecessary stress. You can help them learn healthy ways of coping with unavoidable stress. This will lower their DNQ.

The following questions will help you evaluate your children's DNQ with regard to stress, anxiety level, and coping mechanisms.

Good signs: Do your children know how to relax? Can they keep stress at a reasonable level? Do they ask for support from others? Do they have a support network? Do they use you as a resource?

Bad signs: Do your children seem overly anxious about school? About friends? About relationships in the family? Do their bodies look tense? Do they have sleeping or eating problems? Are they isolated? Are you (the parents) out of the communications loop?

Other considerations: When do your children seem tense? How do they handle it? How do they relax? Are there problems at home that should be addressed to reduce stress? Problems at school? Problems with friends? Other problems?

To reduce your children's drug-neediness with regard to stress and anxiety:

1. *Increase your children's knowledge and awareness of stress, as well as of their own personal indicators of stress.* Start by asking your children if they have heard of the word "stress." They may have some ideas, such as "when things get crazy" or "when I'm under pressure." Explain that stress is the normal response of people to the demands of everyday life. Relate this to their own experiences. Even by kindergarten age, they can understand some of the harsh realities of life: Not everyone will like you. Not all days will be good ones. Sometimes people misunderstand you.

Explain that certain types and levels of stress are good. Sometimes we even choose to take on stress, such as when we try out for a little league team or audition for a school play. But too much stress is unhealthy and makes us feel bad. Explain that we can take actions to reduce stress in our lives. Also, we can learn good ways to cope with it. This is important because people who never learn to cope effectively with stress sometimes turn to drugs, including tobacco, to change and regulate their feelings.

2. *Personalize an understanding of stress.* You can help your children personalize an understanding of stress by teaching

them to recognize stressful events in their lives. Ask them when they experience stress. If they are stuck, make a few guesses: When you have tests in school? When Grandma visits? When you go to Sunday school? When your sister and you fight? When you have nothing to do? When you have too little money? Have your children write a list of what stresses they are experiencing in their life right now. Then you can help them find ways to either reduce the stress or effectively cope with it.

3. *Identify personal signs of stress.* In further personalizing the meaning of stress, teach your children to recognize their own emotional and physical signs. Ask them how they experience stress in their bodies. List possible indicators, such as tight muscles (especially in the neck and jaw), shallow breathing, rapid breathing, whining, irritability, temper outbreaks, lumps in the throat, urges to cry, trembling, difficulty sleeping, sweating hands, feeling weak and tired, headache, upset stomach, feeling helpless, and a racing heartbeat. Explain that when they can recognize the signs of stress, they have a better chance to do something about it.

4. *Teach them how to cope with stress.* Ask your children what they do when they experience stress. Explain that some responses are largely out of their control, such as sweating, but other responses to stress can be controlled. We have options from which to choose—some healthy and others not. Bad options include overeating, taking drugs, smoking cigarettes, or throwing tantrums, all of which only make matters worse. Good options allow us to avoid harm. They resolve, reduce, or replace the stressful state. One of the most effective ways of coping with stress is by solving problems. Another important coping mechanism for children is to ask their parents for support. Tell and remind your children that they can always come to you for help when they need it. You will be their problem-solving partner.

Other coping mechanisms you can teach include finding distractions, such as listening to music or reading a book, and using physical activities for emotional release, such as hitting a punching bag or doing aerobic exercise.

Children can even understand and apply the concept of how we "talk to ourselves." They can give themselves certain encouraging mental messages, such as these: "It will be okay"; "This is hard, but I can handle it"; "I can tough it out"; "This pressure will eventually end"; "I can solve this problem." These sorts of messages encourage endurance and self-confidence.

5. *Discuss family stress.* I recommend a discussion about what causes stress in your own family. With your children, identify and list the sources of stress at home—including major ones such as death, illness, geographic moves, marital problems, or problems with siblings. Consider also the stresses of daily living such as struggles to enforce bedtime, before-school rushes, recurring arguments, housework, report cards, homework, allowance, curfew, or after-school activities. Bringing problems into the open can improve family communication and provide an opportunity for problem solving. Once problems are identified, begin a discussion about how to either eliminate some of the stress or to cope with it better. As a family, you can make an action plan and discuss your progress as you go along.

6. *Go easy on the pressure.* Many middle-class families—including ones with high-achieving parents—excessively pressure and push their children for success, especially in school. This is one of the main complaints I hear from children and teenagers. They say that excellent performance is not encouraged—it is demanded. If their grades are not tops or they are not the star of the soccer team, they feel unappreciated. They often report such a sense of pressure that they cannot turn to their parents for help when they have

problems or suffer ordinary setbacks. When they fall short, parents are disappointed and increase the pressure. I suggest asking yourself these questions: Am I overly demanding about school? Am I overly demanding about achievement? If my children are falling short of my expectations, do I talk with them about the problems, or do I add stress by becoming more demanding and insistent?

Also, many parents are overly punitive—their first reaction to a problem is to punish rather than to become problem-solving partners. When parents punish excessively, children become scared of them. Parents are often unaware of this "scare and punish" dynamic, so I suggest you *really* challenge yourself to consider whether this occurs in your family. If so, I urge you to lighten up. Bear in mind that many adolescents speak of smoking cigarettes or taking other drugs to get relief from the pressures they feel at home.

7. *Teach progressive relaxation.* The two basic physical responses of humans to stress are (1) to tighten muscles and (2) to breath shallowly. Therefore, two good ways to reduce the impact of stress are to learn to relax muscles and to breath deeply. I recommend teaching your children the most basic and easily applied methods of relaxation and deep breathing. This will benefit them throughout life, and also reduce their DNQ.

When I was a young child, my parents introduced me to the method of progressive muscle relaxation, a very easy way to relax oneself. I have used it throughout my life and taught it to countless friends and clients who have used it successfully. You can teach this to your children. First try it yourself. If you don't already do it, I am quite certain you will like it. This is not just folk medicine passed from my parents to me to you. There is substantial research evidence about the benefits of this approach to reducing stress.

Progressive relaxation can be introduced to children as a great way to relax. Explain that you'll go through all the muscle sets in their body from toes to head, asking them to tense up the muscles for a few seconds, and then to relax them. This will help them focus on the pleasant feeling of relaxation. In the end, their whole body will feel relaxed.

Start by asking your children to take off their shoes and to loosen all tight clothing. Tell them to get comfortable in a chair or to lie down, whichever they prefer, with arms and legs uncrossed.

They can begin by taking a couple of deep breaths to relax. Then guide them through their muscle groups.

Here's how the exercise goes:

"Start by tensing up your toes and feet. Curl up the toes. Hold it tight. Feel how tense those muscles are. Good. Good. Hold it for a little bit." After five to seven seconds say, "Now let go and relax your toes and feet. Feel the difference. Feel how relaxed your feet are feeling."

"Now focus on your ankles and calves. Tighten those muscles. Feel how tense they are. Squeeze them tight. Okay. Now hold it. Feel the tension. Good. Good." After five to seven seconds say, "Now let go. Relax those muscles. Feel the release and relaxation. Feel how good it feels. Feel the difference."

People sometimes hold their breath while doing these exercises. This interferes with the relaxation process. Remind your children to continue to breathe. Occasionally suggest that they take a couple of deep breaths.

The next instructions are to tighten the knees and thigh muscles—and to relax them; and then the groin and buttocks (rear, caboose, bottom, or whatever you call this body part in your family).

"As we continue, notice how relaxed you feel from your buttocks down. Pay attention to the lower part of your body. If there is any tension anywhere, go back to that place, tighten your muscles, hold them tight, and then relax. I'll give you a few moments."

Now have your children tense the lower back, stomach, and abdomen—and relax.

Continue to work your way up the body, one set of muscles at a time:

- Squeeze your upper back and chest muscles tight.
- Tighten your shoulders and neck.
- Tighten your arms and clench your hands and fingers— making a fist and squeezing it as tightly as you can.
- Tighten your teeth, mouth, jaw, chin, and lips.
- Close your eyes and squeeze them tight.
- Wrinkle and tighten your forehead and the muscles of your scalp.

Next, ask your children to scan their whole body for tension. If they find any, first they should tighten those muscles, and then relax them. Finally: "Take a few deep breaths and feel how good it is to make yourself relaxed. You can do this exercise any time you want—whenever you feel stressed, even several times a day. Don't get up right away. Relax. Enjoy the feeling. When you are ready to get up, get up slowly."

You can lead your children through this exercise on several occasions, if you want, to help them get started with it.

8. *Teach deep breathing.* The counterpart to relaxing muscles is breathing deeply. Rather than getting complicated about it, I suggest these few simple instructions: Stretch like a cat. Loosen tight clothing. Then get as comfortable as you can get. Lie down on the floor or sink deeply into a chair. Let the muscles in your stomach and abdomen relax. Put one of your hands on your stomach. Gradually take in a nice deep breath through your nose.

Let the air fill your chest and lungs. Let your breath sink lower into your body. You can tell if you are doing this because your chest and abdomen will expand and get bigger. You will feel your hand move on your stomach. When you complete the inhalation, don't hold your breath. Rather, relax your jaw and slowly begin to exhale through your mouth until all the air is gone. Pause at the end of the exhalation. Allow the pause to last until your body wants to inhale again. This has been described as similar to standing on the beach, waiting for the next wave to come in. Then, begin again with a deep breath. Repeat this at least three times. Always inhale through your nose and exhale through your mouth.

Observe your children when they learn this breathing method. People tend to tighten up around their jaw or shoulders. If they do, suggest they let their jaw fall open and allow their shoulders to slump.

Goal III: Emotional Literacy

You want to make sure that your children are emotionally literate. Adolescents and adults often smoke cigarettes to manage their feelings. It is a way to reduce anger and hurt or to counter a negative mood. Teens report smoking when they are angry, upset, hurt, frustrated, "stressed," and bored.

In his book *Achieving Emotional Literacy*, psychologist Claude Steiner wrote that the key elements of emotional literacy include: knowing your own feelings; managing your emotions, including when and how to express them and when to hold them back; having a sense of empathy for others; and knowing how to repair emotional damage, including when and how to apologize and make amends. Finally, emotional literacy involves putting it all together—knowing how to interact successfully with others on an emotional level.

The following questions will help you evaluate your children's DNQ in terms of their skills and deficits in emotional literacy.

Good signs: Do your children seem to be aware of their own feelings? Do they accept them? Can they verbally express their feelings? Can they communicate negative feelings constructively? Can they express affection? Are they open to hearing what others think and feel? Do they seem to care about the feelings of others? Can they apologize sincerely? Can they assertively ask for what they want? Can they accept "no" as an answer? Can they tolerate sadness and other negative feelings?

Bad signs: Do your children seem embarrassed or uncomfortable with emotions? Is their communication inappropriate, aggressive, or ineffective? Are they defensive?

Other considerations: How do they handle anger and resentment? Have they suffered or witnessed any serious abuse? How do they handle disappointment?

The following recommendations describe ways to reduce your children's drug-neediness quotient by increasing their emotional literacy:

1. *Create a home atmosphere of accepting and expressing all feelings.* Be open and honest with your own feelings. Help your children identify and communicate theirs. Pay attention and show interest in what your children feel. Respect their feelings and ask them to respect yours. Be sure to verbally and physically express your love and affection. It is also important to accept your own and your children's negative emotions, such as fear, sadness, and anger.

2. *Teach children to tolerate negative feelings.* Help them understand that they do not need to escape or run away from their feelings. Most feelings of sadness will pass with time. Encourage them to feel strong enough to endure the down periods. Sadness is different from depression, which is a more persistent disturbance and requires attention. Children

also need to learn to endure periods of upsetness. This passing mood is different from chronic upsetness, which results from trauma, and requires attention. Too often adults serve as bad role models when they attempt to escape or run away from negative feeling states instead of showing that one can ride out these moods or, in the case of depression or trauma, triumph over them. We sometimes become overprotective of our children and try to make their bad feelings go away immediately. Learning to tolerate, or resolve, unpleasant feelings is an important skill for kids to develop. Many teenagers who cannot do this turn to tobacco or other drugs to make their feelings go away.

3. *Talk about upsetting events.* There's a fine line between information we should share with children, and what we should withhold. Certainly children should be spared some of the ugly and harsh realities of our world. However, when they have been directly touched by something profoundly disturbing, such as bitter conflict between parents, a divorce, a family member who abuses alcohol or other drugs, the death of a loved one, or other traumas, it is important that you talk about it with them in an age-appropriate manner. They need an opportunity to express their feelings and to process and resolve the impact of these events. If they have been severely traumatized, or require more help than you can give at home, they may need professional services.

4. *Conduct family meetings.* Once a week, try to have a family meeting. Even pre-kindergarten children can use a simple format, such as saying one thing they liked about what happened in the family this week, and one thing they didn't like. As children get older, the discussions can become increasingly sophisticated. Family meetings are also an opportunity for problem solving about important family issues.

5. *Foster a feelings-friendly family by playing a "game" called Telling the Truth.* This game helps your children to appreciate

and accept themselves and their feelings, and to communicate with the family. You present sentence stems, such as those listed below, and give your kids an opportunity to provide their own endings. You can do them one at a time, or a few at a time, on different occasions. It's important to make it safe for your children to say *anything*, so that they can honestly express themselves, and you get an opportunity to know them better. It would be counterproductive if you were to dispute or criticize what is said. Here are some sentence stems:

> I feel good when I . . .
> I feel hurt when I . . .
> I find it hard to . . .
> A good decision I made this week was . . .
> I feel sad when . . .
> I feel scared when . . .
> I feel loved when . . .
> I feel frustrated when . . .
> I feel best with our family when . . .
> I feel best with my friends when . . .
> I get angry when . . .
> I worry most about . . .
> My biggest gripe about school is . . .
> When I think about my schoolwork, I feel . . .
> My one wish is . . .
> My biggest goal is . . .
> My strongest feeling about my brother
> (or sister) is . . .
> The last time I cried was . . .
> What I most want to tell you, Mom (or Dad) is . . .

6. *Use disciplined ways to express negative emotions and teach these methods to your children.* I have written at length on this subject and recommend another book of mine, *Who's on Top,*

Who's on Bottom: How Couples Can Learn to Share Power, if you are interested in thoroughly exploring this topic. But to get started I would suggest adopting a well-regarded format for expressing resentment and other negative emotions. The format is called "I statements" and involves a fill-in-the-blanks sentence that goes like this: *When you did* (A), *I felt* (B).

In this format, (A) is a description of a specific behavior, such as, "When you left the dirty dishes in the sink after dinner" or "When you said I was a bad father." When describing the behavior, it is important to be specific. For example, it is better to say, "When you left crumbs on the kitchen counter and dishes in the sink," than the more general, "When you left a mess in the kitchen." The more specific the speaker is in explaining the behavior, the better the chances are that the listener will understand the event being described. (B) is a description of how you feel now, or felt at the time the event occurred, for example, angry, annoyed, hurt, sad, or scared. The intensity of the feeling can be described with adjectives such as *very, extremely,* and *slightly.* A complete sentence using the format would be, "When you left dirty dishes in the sink after dinner last night, I felt annoyed." Another example would be, "When you raised your voice at me, I felt very hurt and angry."

The beauty of the format is that people get to say how they felt when a specific event occurred without overwhelming, judging, or attacking another person. The statement represents an indisputable expression of emotion, saying essentially, "*When* (A) *happened, this* (B) *is how I felt.*" People who love each other in a family need to know how their actions affect one another. This format provides that information in a nonthreatening way.

Learning to *receive* an "I statement" is also important. The best way to do so is to listen carefully and to acknowledge hearing what was said. People simply need to know that their feelings are being heard. Often that's all it takes to re-solve matters. Sometimes listeners will want to respond immediately. In general, it's best to wait—to prevent defensiveness and to really think about what was said.

Parents who express their feelings with "I statements" serve as role models—taking their own feelings seriously and presenting them in disciplined, respectful ways. Children can and should be taught to use this format. It empowers them to express in words what they feel, including negative emotions about other family members.

People who use this format will want to be careful not to insert judgments into either part of the statement. In the above example, judgments could wrongly have been inserted in either the first or second phrase, as illustrated below:

"*When you acted like a slob*, I felt annoyed."

"When you left dirty dishes on the counter, *I felt that you were being a slob*."

Note that in this last statement, although the words used were "I felt," what followed was a judgment, not a feeling.

When using this format, be careful to avoid exaggeration, especially the use of such terms as "always" and "never" when they do not accurately describe the situation, as in, "When I ask you to do something, you never do it, and I re-sent that." These extreme words often make descriptions of a behavior inaccurate.

Remember that the spirit of this format is to make sure that people feel free to say what they feel and are equally committed to listening to what other family members feel. I cannot overstate the benefit of using communication skills such as this one in family life. An enormous amount of ado-lescent substance abuse is motivated by (a) pent-up emotions that are not communicated and (b) attempts to alleviate the pain that was caused by undisciplined, poor communication.

7. *Make special allowances for your children's frustrations, secret fears, and other feelings and situations that might be bothering them.* Children often feel embarrassed or ashamed about what they feel. They need extra help breaking through communication barriers. They need to be urged and encouraged to talk about what is truly on their minds. Sometimes it helps to guess at their feelings to get them started. For example: I bet you feel hurt that you weren't invited to the party? Is that right? How do you feel? Another example: You seemed upset after school. What happened today? I can see something is bothering you.

Once kids start talking, they may need comfort or help with problem solving.

Goal IV: Mastery

The negative emotions associated with setbacks and frustrations in daily living cause discomfort and are one of the factors that contribute to an urge to smoke. People are anxious, sad, or depressed when things are not going well for them. When problems accumulate and escalate, a fear of failure and sense of defeat can make matters even worse.

Teens say, "I smoke to calm down or when I feel bad." They say, "I smoke when I'm frustrated; when things aren't going right; when school gets to me; when my parents get to me." They say, "Oh, what's the use?" and smoke when they feel hopeless.

An important protection against these negative emotional states is to be successful and to develop the I-can-do-it attitude. This means gaining a sense of personal control and hardiness, which can lower a person's drug-neediness quotient. I refer to this as a *mastery approach* to living. This means that kids are experiencing success in school, in family life, in social relationships, and in all important aspects of their lives. When they suffer setbacks or make mistakes, they have the resilience to stay the course and learn from these experiences.

You want to determine if your children are thriving. The following questions will help you evaluate your children's DNQ in terms of their success in having mastery over life. I suggest you make your own observations first, before directly asking questions.

Good signs: Are your children accepting challenges? Handling frustrations well? Feeling successful and fulfilled in their school work? Social life? Family life? Is their lifestyle healthy? Can they admit shortcomings and mistakes? Are they optimistic about themselves and their lives? Do your children come to you with their fears and problems? Do they seek support from you or other mature people?

Bad signs: Do your children retreat from challenges? Are they defensive? Are they too hard on themselves? Are they unapproachable? Are they feeling helpless or hopeless?

The following recommendations describe what you can do to reduce your children's drug neediness by teaching a mastery approach to living:

1. *Teach your children about mastery living by explaining it to them.* Mastery living means that an individual sets a high standard, continues to seek challenges throughout life, and sticks with them until they are mastered. In the course of these challenges, the setbacks, mistakes, and problems that occur are accepted as part of the process. A person learns from these experiences, gets whatever help or support is needed, and persists with the challenge. You can teach your children about mastery living by explaining it to them, and by creating an environment that supports focus, effort, determination, and success.

2. *Be approachable: Make sure your children feel that they can talk with you about anything.* First, think for yourself whether your children approach you when they are upset or

troubled. Then ask your kids: When you have fears, problems, or complaints, or when you make mistakes, are you able to talk with me about them? If the answer is yes, ask them to tell you their current ones. If the answer is no, ask: What am I doing that makes it feel unsafe? What could I do to make it feel safer? What do you need from me?

If your children cannot come to you with their troubles, where will they turn for support? This is especially important during the teen years when your children will be making important and difficult decisions. If you are deemed unapproachable, you will be excluded from the decision-making process, leaving the peer group as the only major influence.

3. *Show confidence in your children by providing a stimulating environment: Help them set challenging goals and a high standard of conduct.* There is much research indicating that high expectations will foster high performance, provided the goals are attainable and adequate support is available. High achievement might include encouraging your children to learn a musical instrument, play on an athletic team, perform particularly well in school, or make new friends. If you want to foster success, it's important to provide adequate support—whether it means helping them develop sound study habits, teaching skills you know, or driving your children to soccer practice. If the goals are unrealistic, too demanding, or unattainable (see number 5, below), they will be seen as a threat.

4. *Stress the importance of effort, discipline, and perseverance.* Children need to learn that effort is required to master difficult tasks. They often want to be good at something, but need help understanding that it takes a strong effort over a prolonged period of time to gain mastery of complex tasks. Children need to learn to tolerate frustration, solve problems, and persevere with their efforts at mastery.

5. *Praise effort and acknowledge success.* It is most important to praise the *effort* of your children as they strive for suc-

cess. It is prolonged effort, complete with mistakes and set-backs, that ensures mastery. You can acknowledge accomplishments, but be careful not to focus on them exclusively because this could contribute to the belief that all you care about is performance.

6. *Handle mistakes gently.* If you have high expectations for your children—as most of you probably do—you might want to look closely at your reactions to your children's problems. Harsh criticism scares children and undermines their self-esteem. Be gentle when you are critical. Also, teach your children to be self-assured and compassionately self-critical so they can accept the inevitability of mistakes and setbacks, and learn from them. Make sure your children don't take their mistakes and setbacks as indicators of failure, which would lead them to feel embarrassed and defeated.

7. *Be a supportive, problem-solving partner to your children when the going gets rough.* Do not substitute repressive approaches for problem solving. For example, a "bad" report card is too often treated as an occasion for punishment or increasing restrictions. I call it report-card wars. Parents tend to see poor grades as an indicator of laziness or lack of discipline. They attempt to correct the problem by "sentencing" their children to more hours of homework and studying. Anticipating this type of response, children fear their parents and try to hide school problems. A surefire way to lower your "accessibility" rating is to get repressive in response to problems.

Repressive approaches to school disregard the fact that children themselves would very much like to succeed, but might not know how, or may not feel that they can. They might even hide their discouragement by saying that school is boring. What they need instead of punishment is supportive help with problem solving.

A much better response to a substandard report card, or any significant problem, is to be on the same side as the child: to be a problem-solving partner. The message should be: "No problem is too big for us to solve. I'm on your side. I love you and together we can figure this out."

With regard to poor grades, a parent might say: "I imagine you feel pretty discouraged about your report card. Let's talk it over and figure out the problem. I'd like to help you improve your grades if you'd like that."

Usually a parent/child discussion can uncover the underlying problems. Sometimes the answer can be found by simply asking the child. He or she might respond, "I get scared when I take tests." Often the child doesn't know. In these circumstances, you can help by asking questions: Do you have trouble concentrating when you do schoolwork? Which subjects cause you problems? How do you study for exams? Is something upsetting you and interfering with your concentration?

It could be that children are upset about something, even a problem at home, that is distracting them. Perhaps they need help developing study skills—finding a quiet place to do homework or picking a time to do their homework without distractions. They may not understand how to prepare for tests. They may have lost confidence in their abilities. The solution may not be simple, but identifying the real cause of poor grades is, at least, the first step in problem solving. And that is the goal: to stick with the problem until it is solved so that mastery can be attained.

8. *Teach the mastery approach to schoolwork.* I recommend teaching children the mastery approach to education when they first enter school. They should be told the importance of *never falling behind.* When they do not understand a lesson or an assignment, they should always ask questions in class, approach the teacher after class, speak with you (their parents), request a tutor, or do whatever it takes to understand and master the material. The guideline is, "Never stop asking

until you understand the lesson." Children sometimes fear that they will appear stupid if they do not understand something and ask for help. We need to explain that being confused, needing help, or asking questions does not make them stupid. Smart people always need help and always get help. That way they learn the lessons and succeed in school. If a child is already behind in schoolwork, it is essential that a program is devised with the school, using tutors if necessary, to help the child catch up.

Although the conventional wisdom is that drug problems cause school failure, my experience in working with young people has been that many of them have problems in school first, and then turn to tobacco or other drugs to deal with their sense of failure.

9. *Have mastery living discussions with your children.* If you have created an open and safe climate for discussion in the home, then you are in a good position to start mastery discussions with your children. On a regular basis, ask them how they are doing and how they feel about how they are doing in school (academically and behaviorally), at home, and with friends. Encourage them to express any problems, fears, or frustrations they may be experiencing. Offer your perspective and start a discussion.

Your efforts in helping your children learn how to have fun, reduce and cope with stress, increase emotional literacy, and adapt a mastery approach to living will not only reduce their emotional DNQ but will also enable them to thrive in general. In the next chapter, we will discuss ways to lower our kids' social DNQ.

CHAPTER FOUR

Teaching Children to Be Social without Tobacco

An eighteen-year-old girl who wanted to quit smoking told me about her first experience: "I was out with my best friend and two other girls. I was fifteen. One of the girls just got her driver's license. Someone suggested we go to a 'head shop' to see if we could buy cigarettes. We went. They sold us a pack. So we decided to smoke them for a lark."

Seventeen-year-old Michael told me about his first time smoking. He said he used to admire his cousin, who was two years older than he, and smoked. One day when Michael was in the sixth grade, his cousin offered him a cigarette and said: "Dude, you gotta do this." So Michael smoked without any hesitation—and felt cool. "I thought I would barf," he said, "but it went away. I kept trying cigarettes with my cousin a few times before I became a regular smoker." Michael told me that a few years later he offered some other younger kids cigarettes, and remembered saying the same thing: "Dude, this is cool. You gotta do it."

These examples are typical of first use of tobacco. The Surgeon General's Report *Preventing Tobacco Use Among Young People* stated that "peer influence seems to be particularly potent in the early stages of tobacco use; the first tries of cigarettes and smokeless tobacco occur most often with peers, and the peer group may subsequently provide expectations, reinforcement, and cues for experimentation."

The Surgeon General also noted that because adolescence is a time of "multiple transitions," individuals in this stage of life are particularly vulnerable to the lure of tobacco. They may see smoking as a tool that will assist them with these transitions. Those who report that tobacco serves "positive functions" or is "potentially useful" are at increased risk for smoking. To adolescents with low self-esteem, smoking offers both a way to bond with peers and an image that could be attractive to the peer group.

Advertisers exploit the vulnerability of adolescents by implying that tobacco will somehow make their lives better or more enjoyable. In particular, advertising tries to make smoking seem attractive and to suggest that it can be helpful in their social life. Ads also create confusion about the pervasiveness of smoking, making it seem more popular than it is.

Raising Socially Competent Children

Considering the desire of youth to be accepted by peers and the strong influence of peers in the early stages of tobacco initiation, it is essential that we teach young people how to resist social pressure—including the pressures of the tobacco industry itself, as discussed in chapter two. Part of this effort includes correcting misperceptions about the prevalence and social benefits of smoking. Current estimates in the Surgeon General's Report are that 16 percent of twelve- to eighteen-year-olds and 28 percent of high school seniors smoke. In other words, most teenagers *do not* smoke. Furthermore, a recent survey showed that 78 percent of twelve- to seventeen-year-old boys say they prefer to date a nonsmoker. Among girls, 69 percent say they prefer a nonsmoker.

Another very important aspect of helping youth resist social pressure is teaching them resistance skills, discussed in the second part of this chapter. Teaching children to "say no"

has enormous appeal as a simple approach to solving the tobacco problem. It seems so easy: we tell young people that
tobacco is dangerous, and then teach them how to refuse all
offers. However, knowledge of the dangers of tobacco is of
little benefit to individuals who are already committed to
using it because of a high drug-neediness quotient (DNQ).
Their desire to use tobacco overrides their knowledge of its
dangers, and must be reduced before resistance skills can
work.

The impact of social drug-neediness is illustrated well in
the comments of a twenty-four-year-old man who had this to
say about his early history with tobacco: "When I was fourteen I didn't have many friends. I was always nervous around
the other kids. I kept quiet because I was afraid I'd say something stupid. Then one day I stole a pack of cigarettes from
my father, took them to school, and gave them out to some
of the kids who smoked. I smoked with them—trying hard
not to choke or appear stupid. The funny thing is that the
kids who smoked were nice and kind of accepted me. I
started hanging out with them and, of course, smoking.
When I got used to it, the cigarettes made me feel more relaxed around my friends. Hey, I had those drug awareness
classes. I knew how to say no. I knew that tobacco was dangerous, too. But I wanted to fit in. So I said yes, and
smoked."

To keep the social DNQ low, we need to raise socially
competent children who:

1. feel comfortable with peers;
2. can establish and maintain close, meaningful
   friendships; and
3. act as leaders, rather than followers.

Armed with these skills, young people will be less
"needy" for peer acceptance, and therefore less willing to en-

gage in health-compromising behaviors, such as using to-bacco products, in order to be accepted or popular. In other words, they will have the tools to "say no."

Assessing Your Children's Social Skills

You can start by assessing your children's social skills. Then decide which skills need the most reinforcement. Here are some questions to consider when making your assessment.

Good signs: Are your children comfortable in social situations? Do they know how to make friends? Can they maintain friendships? Do they handle conflict well? Can they express their feelings to peers? Are they comfortable with members of both sexes? Do they have leadership qualities?

Bad signs: Are your children isolated and lonely? Do they get nervous with peers? Do they seem too eager for approval? Do they tend to follow the crowd? Do they have unstable and conflict-ridden relationships?

Teaching Social Skills

The best way to reduce your children's social DNQ is by teaching social skills. Here are some suggestions.

1. *Make the teaching of social skills a high priority and an integral part of family life*. The most important proactive measure in this realm is to openly discuss peer relationships with your children. Try to make this discussion a regular part of family life—whether at dinner, before bed, at informal meetings, or at formal family meetings. Inquire about their social life: "Who are you playing with these days? Who are your friends? What do you like about them? What do they like about you? What do you do when you have problems with your friends?" Ask your children for their definition of friendship, and share your own. Ask them: "What makes someone a true friend? What makes a friendship work? What should friends do when they have

disagreements?" Children need ongoing help in learning about social relationships.

2. *Teach children how to make friends and get along with peers.* You can start as early as preschool. In doing this, include basic lessons, such as: telling your name to another child; asking the other child for his or her name; spending time with a new friend; being nice to that child; finding things that you both like to do (common interests); sharing and taking turns; discussing what you are doing together (activities); talking nicely and giving compliments; helping each other out when you need help; asking a friend to play with you at school; inviting a friend to visit at home; telling a friend what you feel; and being fair and talking nicely when you disagree.

3. *Make sure that your children have friends, and if not, figure out what has been the barrier.* Observe your children with other children. See how they get along with others. Watch for little indicators of problems, such as a child's saying: "Nobody likes me. Nobody wants to play with me." See if this is a false perception, in which case reassurance will help, or whether there is a behavioral problem impeding friendship that could be corrected. If your children are isolated, encourage them to make friends and teach them how to do it. Help them select someone with whom they would like to become friends, and then brainstorm together about how to build a friendship.

4. *Teach cooperation and conflict-resolution skills.* Encourage your children to deal with resentment and hurt feelings in direct ways. Teach them practical communication skills for expressing their feelings with peers, such as those discussed in chapter three in the section on emotional literacy. From time to time, give your children opportunities to problem-solve about their friendships. Ask if there is a friend, or group of friends, with whom they are having problems, and help them figure out what they can do.

5. *Help your children identify their own relationship "styles" that may be dysfunctional.* For example, check whether your children tend to withdraw when problems occur; have trouble saying what they really feel; blow up when they get angry; attempt to buy friendships; get overly competitive with friends; get critical and sarcastic. You can discuss your observations and suggest healthier ways of handling relationships.

6. *Teach empathy.* An important way to teach empathy and caring for others is to let your children know your own feelings as they occur, particularly in response to their actions. Too often children are shielded from the impact of their behavior on other family members, and so cannot learn to take another person's perspective.

When your children have conflicts with friends, encourage them to think about how the other person feels. Ask your children what they think the other person is thinking. Talk about the idea of "walking in someone else's shoes."

When children behave aggressively, help them understand that others will not want to play with them. Show them how to make sincere apologies.

Another way to teach empathy is to have your children think about less fortunate people. For example, you can ask them what they think it feels like to live in poverty, with very little money for food and many people crowded in a small living space. Or ask them to think about life in a family with a problem drinker. In such a family, children never know what to expect from the intoxicated parent and might be embarrassed, or even scared, to invite friends to visit. On a more positive note, as a family, you can demonstrate empathy by contributing to a food bank, volunteering at a soup kitchen, or supporting an important social cause.

7. *Help your children gain self-assurance and leadership skills.* Social influence works on your children long before they are old enough to be tempted by drugs. You can see the

effects of social influence in the latest toy crazes, trendy television shows, fad movies, and gifts that become the rage each Christmas. Advertisers know about the power of social influence. They use the bandwagon effect to sell their products by implying that "everybody's doing it" or "everybody needs this." If we are to protect our children from this sort of influence, then before we teach them to say no to drugs, we should help them develop independent minds and opinions, and a strong sense of self.

One way to teach this is by serving as role models. For example: When all the other parents allow their kids to watch violent shows, such as the *Power Rangers*, you as parents can be a model of independence by resisting it. So what if you are the only parents bucking the trend! Explain to your children why you oppose these particular shows. Even if your children would prefer to be watching them, you can help them feel proud about being part of the minority. Show your children how to "go against the crowd." Talk about the good feelings you get when you stick up for what you believe.

Independent-minded young children develop their own tastes, opinions, and preferences. Help them know their own positions by asking questions such as these: What is your favorite color? What do you like to do best for fun? What is your favorite toy? What did you like best about what happened this week in our family? What did you like least? What was the best thing that happened in school today? Was there anything that bothered you?

To nurture their critical thinking abilities, children can be encouraged to formulate and express their opinions about family, community, and world affairs. Children who know who they are, and where they stand, are far less likely to be swayed by a group of peers headed in a negative direction.

8. *Increase your children's level of comfort in social situations.* Ask your children how they feel when they meet new peers, or

attend parties, or when they spend time with friends. Explain that it is normal to feel some degree of anxiety in social situations, especially with new people and in new situations. However, people can get anxious to an unhealthy degree. It's important to be able to relax, be ourselves, and trust that most people will find us likable. You can have your children practice a variety of behaviors that will help them feel more comfortable in social situations, such as engaging in small talk, making phone calls, asking for directions, greeting people with hellos, asking for help from teachers, starting conversations in a store while shopping, and giving compliments. Urge your children to speak out in these ways, even if it makes them nervous. They'll see that practice makes it easier.

Building Your Children's Resistance Skills

Children who know how to start and maintain successful relationships, as discussed above, will feel comfortable with peers. They will not be as "needy" for friends or social approval. This affords them a degree of independence and puts them in an ideal position to benefit from resistance skills—the skills needed to resist social pressure, including pressure to use tobacco products. Resistance skills are actually part of a broader category of behavior known as "assertiveness" that you will want to teach your children. Assertive individuals are self-assured, can express their thoughts and feelings openly and honestly, and can "stick to their guns." Boosting your children's resistance skills and overall assertiveness will not only reduce the odds of tobacco addiction, but also serve as an investment in raising strong, independent individuals.

I suggest you talk with your children about the concept of assertiveness, and contrast it with passive behavior, which occurs when people ignore what is on their minds or give in to pressure from others.

Have your children identify situations in which they were unable to stand up for themselves, for example when they were overlooked by a sales clerk in a department store, or when they couldn't ask a friend for a favor, or when they didn't say that they disagreed with something that one friend said about another friend. Maybe there were times when they didn't stick up for themselves with you, their parents. Ask them to discuss these situations. Brainstorm a list of reasons that keep people from behaving assertively, including ones such as these:

- They worry about making a "scene."
- They want to avoid a fight.
- They are embarrassed.
- They are frightened.
- They don't want to look foolish.
- They don't want to offend the other person.

Finally, help your children understand the great importance of learning to be assertive. Assertiveness allows us to:

- bring problems into the open,
- resolve problems,
- feel good about ourselves because we are strong and honest,
- increase our chances of getting what we want out of life, and
- gain the respect of others who see us as self-assured.

Peer Influence

Explain to your kids that it is sometimes difficult for people to be assertive when a peer, or group of peers, is involved. We all want to have friends and want to be liked. It's normal to be concerned about, and influenced by, what others think and feel. However, we can go too far in seeking peer acceptance and approval.

This discussion can be made more concrete by using an example such as this: "Suppose several friends told you that you looked good in a certain type of sweater. How would you feel? How would it affect your choices of the clothing you wear? Now suppose that they said you looked bad in a certain color? How would you feel? How would it affect the way you dressed?" These questions point to the subtleties of peer influence. Too often, we think of peer pressure only in its most overt and obvious forms—when one person bullies another into doing something against his or her will. Although this sometimes occurs, most peer influence is more subtle and indirect, such as when someone hands out cigarettes to a group of teens, and everyone takes one. In such a situation, young people feel unspoken pressure to conform.

Tell your children a peer pressure story such as the following true one, and use it to discuss "going along with the crowd":

> At recess some of the second-grade girls in school would hide under the steps instead of going to the playground where they were supposed to go. Christina knew it was wrong and didn't want to get in trouble. It didn't even seem like fun to her. But one day, one of the girls said, "C'mon, Christina. We're going under the steps." Another girl said, "You look scared. What, are you a chicken?" Christina didn't want to hide with the other girls but went anyway.

Ask your children: "What do you think swayed her to go? What do you imagine she was thinking at the time? What was she feeling?"

Younger kids may give very simple answers: "Christina went because she didn't want to be called names." Older kids can give more sophisticated explanations. This exercise leads easily to a discussion of the tactics, known as "power plays," in which people try to control the behavior of others. You and your children can brainstorm a list of power plays, such as sulking; relentless nagging; brute force; the threat of force; the threat of harm; guilt; teasing; daring; promising rewards; flattery; shunning; rejection; and the use of logic to outtalk someone. You can ask your children to reflect on the tactics used by their group of peers to influence behavior.

When I asked my oldest son, then in third grade, about power plays and explained the concept, he listed these tactics:

- when someone makes fun of you
- when people say, "Do it my way or you can't play"
- when people say, "I'll hurt you"
- hitting
- cheating on rules

When I explained some subtler and more indirect power plays, such as crying or threatening to "not like" someone, he was interested and easily understood the concepts.

In teaching assertiveness and resistance skills, we want to help our children know where they stand, and recognize situations in which they are being pressured.

Sensitive children are sometimes passive because they don't want to be aggressive, and do not see an alternative. They make no distinction between assertiveness and aggressiveness. You can clarify the difference: Aggressive behavior means overreacting, hurting, attacking, and sometimes injuring others. Assertiveness is about people standing up for themselves and their beliefs—expressing their thoughts and feelings and making free choices—but without violating the rights of others.

Role-Playing Assertiveness

You should teach your kids assertiveness skills early because by the fifth grade, many of them already report having
been offered alcohol, tobacco, or other drugs. The best way
to teach assertiveness is through role playing. You and your
children can have a good time with this. I suggest beginning
with easy situations. Parents and children can take turns
playing the "troublemaker" and the assertive person. Work
on general assertiveness first, and tobacco-related role-plays
later.

Role playing is best when you set the scene well. That is,
you establish a setting, put characters in positions that would
match real life (such as near or distant to one another, standing or sitting, etc.), discuss the mood of the characters, and
perhaps give the starting sentence.

Here is an example of a role-play with an eight-year-old
child:

"Your best friend is visiting. You're in your room. I'll play
your best friend. I'm sitting here, on this chair, which we can
make believe is the chair in your room. You're sitting on the
floor, right next to me, playing with your toy castle. Okay, sit
down on the floor here, next to me, and pretend you're playing with the castle. As your best friend, I'll say something
cruel about your sister, Elaine. In this role-play, my statement bothers you, and you want to say something about it.
Practice speaking your mind to me. Get it? Understand the
scene?"

"Yes."

"Are you ready?"

"Yes."

"Okay, I'll go first and then you answer. Here goes: I
think Elaine is really stupid the way she always wants to play
with us. She's a creep."

(Then the role-play unfolds.)

In role playing, people tend to get "out of role" to explain something or cut the tension. Try to avoid this diversion. Try to stay in character and complete the scene, and then have a discussion afterward.

In coaching your children, remind them that being assertive means stating your position and possibly the reason for your position. Tell your children that assertiveness applies to both the words and the behavior of an individual. Help them with body language as well as verbal skills. Coach them on loudness of voice, eye contact, facial expression, body posture, and physical distance.

The best role-plays will be of age-appropriate situations that your children are likely to encounter. You know your children best and can make your own choices about what is most relevant.

There are two ways to do these role-plays. One is to select a situation and simply practice various responses, including assertive ones. If your children cannot spontaneously think of assertive responses to a situation, you can help them with it. The other way is to use the same situation, but to first problem-solve about possible responses. Ask your children about the situation: What would you feel? What would you want to say or do? What do you think you would actually say or do? What would be an assertive response? Then you role-play the scene. Here is an example:

- "At a food court in a shopping mall, some of the kids say "pizza" and start walking toward the pizza restaurant. You would rather a different choice. What would you feel? What would you say? What would you do?" Ask your children to role-play this situation the way they would probably respond. If the response is not an assertive one, say: "Now role-play it assertively, trying to establish your preference. Try to be an independent person or a leader, but don't be aggressive."

More scenarios to role-play assertiveness:

- In the schoolyard, your friends are planning an adventure. They are not including a new kid in school. You want to suggest including this new kid.
- A friend makes a racist remark about members of a minority group. You are offended.
- You heard that a "friend" is saying nasty things about you. You're not sure, but you want to ask your friend about it.
- The teacher has explained a lesson and is about to move on to something new. You are still confused. It appears that most of the other students have understood the lesson. You would like to ask a question.
- Your friends are being nasty to another kid. You don't like it.
- (For an adolescent with a driver's license) You're driving the family car. Your parents do not allow anyone to smoke in the car because of the smell. Some friends in the back seat start to light up cigarettes. You know the car will smell bad if they smoke.

Some of these scenes can be repeated, with you and your children swapping roles. The playfulness of this experience creates a relaxed feeling and provides an opportunity for personal disclosure. You can talk about some of the peer pressure you experienced as a child and that you now experience as an adult. You can give your own opinions about the best ways to resist peer pressure.

Ways to Say No

As you can see, assertive behavior is appropriate in a wide variety of situations. Now let's discuss a special type of assertiveness—saying no—also known as refusal skills. You can give your children practice in saying no to various scenarios, including some involving tobacco or other drugs.

When it comes to tobacco, it has been found that a clear family position against the use of tobacco products helps support a child in resisting peer pressure. Research also indicates that resistance skills are most helpful when they are reviewed and practiced repeatedly.

Two key guidelines have been identified about helping your children say no:

1. Help them develop simple responses and provide them with exact phrases that they may want to use. (Different ways to "say no" are listed in the next section of this chapter.)
2. Teach assertive "refusals" that allow your children to "save face," have fun, and keep their friends.
   Example: When friends propose getting cigarettes from a convenience store, good face-saving responses might be either of the following:
   "Actually I have other things I want to do."
   "Why don't we go to the community center? I heard they have a great band tonight."
   These statements often work better than an extreme one, such as:
   "That's dumb. I don't want to have anything to do with it."

Below are some situations you could role-play with your children to practice refusal skills.

- Someone asks to copy your homework. It will be obvious that it was copied. You want to say no.
- A friend who is always late asks if you would pick her up to go to a ball game. You don't want to pick her up because you don't want to be late.
- You're in a store with friends who start stealing stuff. You don't want to steal anything and you don't want to get in trouble with them.

- Kids are playing with lighters and matches at a friend's house. You don't want to do it.
- One boy is handing out cigarettes to a group of boys and girls. You'll be next. Everyone is accepting the offer. You don't want to smoke.
- A good friend *challenges* you to smoke a cigarette while you are with a group of friends.
- You're with a bunch of guys who all want to chew tobacco. They've got a pouch of it. The thought of chewing tobacco makes you sick to your stomach.

Below is a list of ways to say no, organized into various categories, that could provide a basis for a family discussion to evaluate their respective merit and to identify personal preferences:

Simple refusals:

No thank you.
I don't feel like it.
I don't want to.
I'll pass.

Bigger refusals:

I don't smoke.
It's not for me. I'm just not interested in smoking.

Changing direction:

Let's go to the mall instead.
I'd rather play basketball.

Making excuses:

I have a cough.
I don't feel well.
It's a habit I can't afford.

I'm too busy.
I'm on my way to the store.
My coach won't let me.
I want to stay in athletic shape.

Leaving the scene:

(Walk out.)
(Go for walk.)
Gotta get home.
No thanks, bye.

Leaving the door open:

I can't stay now. But I'll catch up with you later.

Using humor:

No, if I'm lucky, my girlfriend (boyfriend) might be smelling my breath later.

Opposing the proposed behavior:

It's not very smart.
It's bad for you.
It'll just get me in trouble.
No way.

Avoiding High-Risk Situations

One way to resist negative peer pressure is to avoid getting into situations where the pressure will be intense. Sometimes children know ahead of time when a group of friends are headed for trouble. It's easier to bail out sooner than later. Here's an example you could try with your child:

"You're with a group of friends after school and they're going to someone's house where no parent is home. They want to get beer from the refrigerator and smoke cigarettes. It appears that everyone is going."

Here are some questions to ask: "What would you feel? What would you want to say? What would you want to do? If you didn't want to go, do you think you could say so? Could you leave? Why? Why not?"

Then the next task: "Now let's role-play an assertive refusal. Make believe I'm one of the friends. I'll start by saying, "Let's go. Are you ready?""

This is good practice in assertiveness and helps children learn to anticipate high-pressure situations during the "early stages" of trouble.

Putting It All Together: Real-Life Role Playing

The best role-plays represent real-life situations about which your children need help. If you take an active approach to teaching social skills, you will be discussing peer-related issues with your children from a young age and will find many situations suitable for role playing.

This is what happened in one family with excellent parent/child communication. Matthew, a second-grader, complained after school that he had had a "bad day." His parents asked what was wrong. "I hate recess," was the answer. He explained that on this day, like almost every other day, one of the bigger, more aggressive boys, Elliot, brought his basketball and then chose who would play on each team. Elliot always put himself on a team with just a few players and pitted them against a larger group. Because one team was so large, many of the boys on that team hardly got to touch the ball. It ruined the fun.

Matthew and his parents discussed options such as insisting on different teams; bringing his own basketball and starting his own game; or inviting some of his friends to play another sport.

After a discussion, Matthew said he wanted to stand up to Elliot. He and his parents role-played the situation. First he rehearsed what he would say to some of the other boys before recess. He said: "Today I think we should have someone else pick the teams, besides Elliot. It's not fair when he picks the teams. Don't you think so?" In the role-play, he got his friends' agreement. Next he rehearsed what he would say on the playground:

"I don't think it's fair that Elliot picks the teams each day. The teams are never fair. I think that we should have two captains and they should take turns picking players."

What happened the next day was surprising. Matthew talked to a couple of friends. They all decided not to play basketball. The anticipated showdown with Elliot didn't happen. That night and as the situation unfolded, Matthew got additional guidance at home. Over the next couple of weeks, Matthew and his friends sometimes brought their own basketball to school and started their own game. Most kids joined with them. Elliot wanted to play, too, and tried to dominate this new game. But Matthew and his friends stood their ground. Finally, Elliot accepted the idea of team captains, and the basketball problem was solved. This was excellent leadership training and a good lesson in assertiveness for Matthew. It was also a wonderful example of how to use positive peer support to accomplish personal goals.

Positive Peer Support

A discussion of resisting negative peer pressure would be incomplete without discussing the other side of the coin: positive peer support. This is exactly what Matthew used to solve his basketball problems. Explain to your children that when they make decisions about what they want to do, it is often helpful to have the support of peers. Instead of being directed by peers to do things they don't want to do, strong individuals use the support of their peers to accomplish the things they do want. This is not a sign of weakness. We really need other people. But, as you have been discussing with your children, we must first be sure of ourselves and know what we want to do. Matthew, with his basketball dilemma, clarified what he wanted to accomplish and then rallied his friends for support.

■ CHAPTER FIVE ■

Talking with
Teens about Tobacco

"My daughter is fourteen and I'm scared." These were the opening remarks of a mother at a parenting workshop. She continued: "Some of my daughter's friends are already having sex. Some are sleeping around. Some of them are smoking, drinking, and doing drugs. What I really feel like doing is keeping her home with me. But when I pull in the reins, she just fights me."

When children become adolescents, many parents get the jitters, just as this mom did, and try to become *more* controlling of their children's behavior. This usually backfires and breeds rebellion, because this is a time in life when young people need to spread their wings and form their own independent identities. Instead of telling adolescents what to do, we should help them learn to think for themselves. What they need is more freedom, not less, combined with good guidance and supervision. In return, we should expect increasingly responsible behavior from our children. Scary? Yes. Nevertheless, it is our job, as parents, to help adolescents develop rational thinking skills so that they can make their own wise decisions and be prepared for young adulthood.

One of the best ways to be sure that freedom is handled responsibly is to raise children who can take care of themselves and meet their needs *without using drugs*. During the teen years, it's important to continue to teach your children how to have fun in healthy ways, how to solve problems to reduce stress, how to cope with stress, how to manage their emotions, and how to master life's challenges.

The Exchange-of-Information Process

By the teen years, all of our tobacco prevention education should be interactive. That is, it should involve a respectful dialogue between parents and children. We need to share ideas, express our thoughts and feelings, and listen to those of our adolescent children. In my book *Saying No Is Not Enough*, I introduced the "exchange-of-information" process, a model for conducting this dialogue in a disciplined way. This process incorporates parental input while encouraging children to think for themselves and to make wise decisions. It involves more than an exchange of information but is named in this way to focus squarely on the need for parents and teenagers to be *rational*, even though they are discussing issues that are emotionally charged.

The exchange-of-information model has five parts:

1. Children and parents agree to have a discussion about tobacco.
2. Parents present their point of view.
3. Children present their point of view.
4. They discuss each other's point of view.
5. Parents and children reach an understanding and make agreements with one another.

Parents are sometimes worried that this model sounds too democratic. They say, "I'm the adult, I set the rules. I don't want to negotiate with my children." I quite agree that we must recognize the distinction between parent and child. I'm not suggesting that parents abrogate their responsibilities, especially in such an important matter as the use of tobacco. However, I am suggesting that when children become adolescents, we can no longer get away with simply laying down the law. We must involve them in a discussion. If we discount their thinking, we will find ourselves in power struggles. The dialogue will come to a grinding halt. When this happens, we will no longer know what our children are thinking or doing. We cannot help advance their thinking or influence their behavior. In contrast, we do *not* surrender our authority nor lose our influence when we agree to respectfully listen to our children and to strive for mutual understanding.

Another way that parents end the dialogue and lose their influence is by listening as long as they like what they hear, but then hitting the roof when they hear something they don't like. Adolescents respond to this aggressiveness by hiding the truth. They begin to say only what they believe their parents "want to hear."

The key to effectively influencing the behavior of adolescent children is to use an educational approach: to create and maintain dialogue. Adolescents benefit from the adult perspective. Parents benefit by better understanding their children. Good discussions increase mutual understanding and can lead to agreements when none seemed possible. When agreements are made after a thorough discussion, children feel a sense of ownership in the outcome and are likely to abide by the terms they helped establish.

Sometimes, however, parents and children cannot reconcile their differing points of view. In these situations, parents maintain their authority and can still establish rules. Of course they must weigh the risks of establishing rules that may be unenforceable or could increase the possibility of rebellious defiance. Nevertheless, compared to times when rules are made arbitrarily without discussion, adolescents are much more likely to abide by the parental "bottom line" if they feel that their parents have listened to them.

Opening the Dialogue

When I suggest families conduct a dialogue about tobacco, parents often ask if I think their children will tell the truth. The answer is quite simple: children who are afraid of their parents probably will not. Those who feel safe probably will. That is why, from the earliest years, it is best to avoid overreliance on punishment. Instead, I recommend the idea of being *problem-solving partners* (previously discussed in chapter three).

I recommend you start by flat-out asking your children if they feel safe enough to tell you the truth about where they stand on tobacco—even if they thought you might not like what you hear. Then I would be specific. "If you felt like smoking tobacco or using any other drug, or if you have already been using them, could you tell me?"

If the answer is "no"—or if it is a glib or unbelievable "yes"—then I suggest you backtrack. Drop the tobacco issue and work first on creating a family climate in which your children feel that they can talk with you about this sensitive topic. Ask them what keeps them from telling you the truth about themselves.

I understand this is not a simple matter. You must be willing to hear criticism. Your adolescent children might tell you that you have been too quick to punish, too dogmatic, too restrictive, too scary, too angry, too out of touch, too much of a lecturer. They are not the final arbiter of the truth, nor of your behavior. But it is important to listen to them.

Parents who have relied heavily on punishment will probably find it difficult to get their children to talk honestly.

If your children do not feel safe talking with you about important issues, you will be excluded from their decision-making process. You *must* find a way to change the climate at home and start a dialogue. If you want honesty, you will have to retreat from trying to control their behavior, and increase your reliance on a strategy of education and persuasion.

The bottom line is this: An investment in creating a family climate of openness and safety is an investment in your entire child-rearing endeavor. Even if it takes months, it is well worth the time and energy. If your children don't talk with you about their behavior, your parental influence will decline. This applies to tobacco, other drugs, sex—and any other wild ideas they may have.

Once you've established a situation in which your children can talk with you openly and honestly, you can then move on to the next step, which is to start a give-and-take exchange about tobacco. To do this, you must guarantee "immunity"; that is, guarantee you will not now, nor in the future when you might be upset with your children, punish them for what they tell you in this discussion.

Presenting Your Point of View

Someone has to go first in a family discussion of tobacco. I suggest you let your children decide. Usually they want their parents to start, so be prepared with your point of view. This is how I would begin:

"Tobacco is a powerful drug. Lots of people smoke because they want to get something good from it. And they think that they won't be harmed. Personally, I believe it's very dangerous. And it makes me really mad that the tobacco industry has aimed its advertising at kids. They make it seem that you'll have fun, be popular, and be relaxed if you smoke their drug. They want to make money and don't care about your health.

"I know this is a very exciting time in your life and that part of the fun is experimenting and trying out different things. That's one reason why so many young people try tobacco. They're curious. They see their friends using it, and it's a huge big deal. It's a way to hang out and connect with other kids.

"I want to be honest with you: some people really like the effect of this drug. They use it to calm down. They use it to get a little burst of energy. Unfortunately, that's the hook. They like it. So they do it a little more. Then a little more. Then still more. They never think they're going to get addicted, *but they do.* Tobacco is very addictive. Addiction sneaks up on people. That's why I feel so strongly that this is a drug to avoid. That's why I think the best bet, if you haven't tried tobacco, is to stay away from it altogether.

"If you've already used tobacco or plan to use it, I hope you can talk with me about it. I want to hear your thinking and discuss it with you. It's important we hear each other out, even if we disagree. I won't punish you for anything you think or feel about tobacco, or for anything you have done with it."

I would stop at this point, remembering that this is the beginning of a dialogue, and not a one-shot discussion. There is plenty of time later to fill in gaps and to make agreements.

What you especially want to guard against in your remarks is what I call "conversation stoppers," which are extreme statements that either threaten or belittle people who use tobacco or consider using it. For example:

- "Anyone who smokes cigarettes would have to be crazy."
- "Anyone who even thinks about smoking is stupid."
- "If I ever find out that you are using tobacco, you'll be in big trouble."

Listening

Now it's time for your children to speak. Ask for their thoughts and feelings. Be sure to say that you want to hear the truth—not what they think you *want* to hear—and that you will be open-minded. Listen carefully. Stay curious. This is an opportunity to understand your children better. Do not interrupt and definitely do not create a rebuttal cycle, in which you try to argue against whatever is said.

One technique for good listening is to pause and think about what you heard *before* responding. This prevents interruptions and reduces defensiveness. Another technique for good listening is to paraphrase what was said: "Let me see if I understand you. It sounds as though you feel . . ." When paraphrasing, you do not agree, disagree, or interpret. You simply feed back what you thought was said to see if you understood it correctly.

Some Children Say Tobacco Is Stupid

If you start your discussion early enough, a great many young adolescents will tell you that they have not smoked, do not intend to use tobacco, and think that using tobacco is stupid. As reassuring as it sounds, this type of statement reveals very little about your children's underlying thoughts. I would caution against inaction. It's important to talk anyway. You need to continue the dialogue to expand their thinking and add depth to their reasons for rejecting this drug. Ask them *why* they think tobacco is stupid.

When adolescents reject tobacco, I think it's quite important to ask them if they realize that many smokers (and chewers) use this drug because they like the way it feels and think it is cool. Some parents worry that this might *encourage* children to use tobacco. On the contrary, these facts should be brought into the open. There is a real lure to drugs—sooner or later your children will become aware of it. We don't have to hide the truth. This is a good time to catch their attention, when they're not even inclined toward drug use. Full disclosure by parents at this point gives you credibility for future discussions. Later, when your children might be more interested in experimenting, they will recognize that you are open-minded and feel that they can be honest with you. If you fail to mention the benefits of tobacco, you will seem naive or narrow-minded to them and may appear unavailable or too rigid in your thinking.

But what if your children ask: "So then, if tobacco is so good, why shouldn't I smoke it (or use smokeless tobacco)?" You can use this sort of an inquiry as an opportunity to (1) review the consequences and dangers of tobacco, and (2) explain that there are healthier ways of attaining the same benefits. Remember, the goal of the dialogue is to promote thinking. If a child mindlessly rejects tobacco as "stupid" one day, he or she may mindlessly think it is "super" or "cool" a short time later. We want our children to think. It is in their best interest to weigh the positive against the negative. We don't have to hide the positive, because we are confident that the cost, if understood, far outweighs the benefits.

If your children seem "anti-tobacco," you can still promote discussion with questions such as these:

- What are your reasons for not using tobacco?
- Do you know kids who smoke?
- Why do you think they smoke?
- How has it affected them? How do you think it might affect their future?
- Have you been offered tobacco?
- If so, what did you feel? What did you say? What did you do? What would you feel, say, and do if you were offered tobacco now?

• What would you do if a friend tried to push you into
trying tobacco? What if someone said, "Hey, don't be
so scared—it's cool."

These questions can expand your children's consciousness and will help you assess both their knowledge of the
topic and their ability to resist peer pressure.

I also suggest saying something like this to leave the door
open: "Even though you know I think tobacco is a dangerous
drug, I hope if you ever change your mind and start to think
that you might want to smoke, you would talk with me about
it." And to open the door still wider, I would add: "You
know, I hope you'll never even try tobacco. But if you ever do
try it, sometime in the future, I hope you'll talk with me
about it."

How *Not* to React to What You Hear

Let's say your child admits to smoking, or admits that
he or she is considering the possibility. When this happens,
you may waver on your solemn pledge to remain calm and
supportive, while you indulge in a "Rambo parenting" fantasy, characterized by an overpowering campaign of disapproval and punishment. The biggest problems with this
fantasy are that:

1. Punishment and disapproval do not address the underlying issue of what is motivating the use of or desire to use tobacco products.
2. When parents overreact, teenage children shut down
   and do not speak honestly with them anymore, thus
   ending the educational influence of parents.
3. Punishment and disapproval usually generate bitter feelings, and increased opposition and resistance.

I suggest great caution: don't overreact to what you hear. You are beginning an educational process. Take responsibility for calming yourself down so that you can have a successful dialogue.

Over and over again I have seen parents panic and hit the roof at the first sign of something they didn't like about the behavior of their adolescent children. Sometimes they responded with excessive punishment. Sometimes they communicated such intense disapproval that their children felt alienated and simply backed away from them. Keep in mind that 70 percent of adolescents try smoking. Many adolescents try smokeless tobacco. Adolescence is a time of exploration. Like it or not, they may be tempted to try tobacco. We can strongly urge against its use and educate about the dangers, but kids will be learning to make their own choices. Part of that learning comes from making mistakes. We can't prevent inevitable mistakes but can help our children learn from them. That's why dialogue is so important.

Our job is to help our children always do better. We want to be available for guidance at times such as these, which are when they need us most. Children feel let down by parents who overreact and essentially take themselves out of the picture. Many times I have heard teens say things like: "You think what I've done is so bad! You've got no clue about what's normal. If you want to see bad—I'll show you bad." And that they do! This sort of interaction foreshadows *really serious* problems in a family.

Helpful Ways to React to What You Hear

My main guideline about responding to discomforting information in a discussion about tobacco or any other emotionally charged topic is to take a deep breath and relax, or at least maintain an air of calmness, even as your heartbeat accelerates and your blood pressure rises. Why not start by expressing appreciation for honesty: "I'm glad you could tell me the truth. Thank you."

To children who are thinking about smoking but haven't, you could express your concern about tobacco, and your hope that now they will begin a thoughtful and thorough discussion with you.

To children who have already tried tobacco, you could also express your concern, but without any put-downs or criticism. For example: "To be completely honest with you, I must tell you that it worries me that you're smoking cigarettes (or chewing tobacco) because I think tobacco is such a dangerous drug. But I'm not going to hit the roof or anything. I just want us to talk about it openly and honestly."

The immediate reaction of your children might be: "Don't worry—I know what I'm doing. It's no big deal. I don't smoke so much, a lot less than any of my friends. I could stop whenever I want. It's my life, not yours."

If you get this reaction, don't engage in a power struggle. Roll with the resistance. As the saying goes, "Don't put your sail in their wind." I suggest you simply acknowledge your children's point of view and push on with the discussion. For example: "You're right—it's your life, not mine. I was just telling you how I feel. I'm glad you have such confidence in yourself. Let's keep talking so we can understand each other better."

This allows you to become a problem-solving partner rather than an antagonist.

Information Gathering

When you ask questions to understand your children's point of view, be careful not to cross-examine or pump them for information. Don't try to find out everything the first time you talk. I suggest you think of information gathering as an ongoing process and keep in mind that the dialogue will continue over time. Keep it relaxed. Keep your sense of humor. You can start with simple, open-ended statements or questions such as these:

"So, tell me more about your use of tobacco."

"What has it been like smoking cigarettes?"

"What are your thoughts about tobacco these days?"

As the discussion unfolds, you will develop a sense of how much questioning is appropriate with your children, and when you need to lighten up or back off. If your children indicate that they can't talk, or feel too pressured at the moment, show that you're not pushy. Sometimes it helps to be encouraging: "I know it's hard for you to talk about this with me, but I think it's important. Please hang in there." At other times it makes more sense to back off: "I think this discussion is getting too intense. Why don't we stop for a while and take a break. We can talk more tomorrow, maybe after dinner. How 'bout it?"

The Stages of Tobacco Use—How to Intervene

As the discussion continues, you will want to determine if your children are merely contemplating the use of tobacco or whether they are beyond that point. If beyond it, you will want to know their stage of tobacco use and how committed they are to continuing with their use (strongly committed, weakly committed, or not committed at all). It is also important to gauge your children's knowledge and level of concern about the consequences and potential harm from the use of tobacco.

The stages of tobacco use are as follows:

Children who have not tried tobacco but are contemplating its use are in the *preparatory stage.*

Children who have only smoked two or three times are in the *trying stage.*

Children who have smoked repeatedly, but on an irregular basis, are in the *experimental stage.*

Children who have smoked at least weekly, and increasingly across a variety of situations and personal interactions, are in the *regular-use stage.*

Children who have developed a tolerance for tobacco (need more of it for the same effect) and manifest withdrawal symptoms when they are not smoking are in the *dependent or addicted stage* of tobacco use. For them, it is no longer a matter of prevention.

Once you determine the stage of smoking that best describes your child, the paragraphs below can help guide your discussion. They list some of the information you will want to gather, and the key points to present over the course of the dialogue. Depending on your child's stage of smoking, refer to the heading below that is most appropriate for you: The Preparatory Stage, The Trying Stage, The Experimental Stage, or The Regular-Use Stage. For help with addicted smokers, I refer you ahead to chapters six, seven, and eight.

The Preparatory Stage

Key points: Find out why your children are tempted to use tobacco. Is it for fun, for excitement, because friends are doing it, for curiosity, or what? Validate the temptation. For example, "I could see why this would be tempting." But then review the consequences and dangers of tobacco use and help them consider the most relevant personal reasons for resisting the temptation. Discuss the value of maintaining the barrier of "never-having-tried tobacco," and suggest they avoid crossing the line. Explore and discuss what would get them to smoke. Explore and discuss what it would take to get them to stop before they start. You can also correct misconceptions they may have about the numbers of young people who smoke.

Questions you will want answered over the course of time include:

- When did you start thinking about using tobacco?
- What is it about tobacco that makes it attractive or tempting?
- What are your worries and concerns about tobacco?
- What has kept you from smoking (or chewing) up to this point?
- What could get you to cross the line to try tobacco?
- What if a friend offered you a cigarette (or chewing tobacco)? Would you smoke (chew)? Why?
- Do you think you will be smoking (or chewing) soon? Six months from now? How about in a year?
- What's next? What can you do to keep yourself from smoking? What can I do to help you resist the temptation?

The Trying Stage

Key points: You can ask why they tried tobacco: Were they curious, seeking an adventure, talked into it by peers, or what? Validate their reasons. For example, "I can see why you were attracted to this." But then, let them know that many people never go beyond this point of "trying" tobacco, and that you hope they will consider quitting now, the easiest time. The more they use it, the harder it will be to quit. Explore and discuss what would get them to continue smoking and what would get them to stop. Another important point to emphasize with them is that experimentation (the next stage of tobacco use) is generally a response to particular situations (such as a party) or to a particular person (such as a best friend). They can think about when, where, and with whom they would be tempted to smoke. You could suggest they consider this: Without a decision to stop, they might be swept along into the next stage of tobacco use if the "right" situations occur. Therefore, it is worth deciding ahead of time whether they want to put an end to this or not. If they want to end it, help them think about how they would handle tempting situations.

Questions you will want answered over the course of time include:

- Why did you first want to try it?
- When did you try it?
- What did you think of the experience?
- Did you like tobacco?
- If yes, what did you like?
- If no, what didn't you like?
- How do you now feel about having used tobacco?
- What are your worries and concerns about tobacco?
- Who was with you when you smoked (or chewed)? What if tobacco were available again?
- What's next: What are your thoughts and attitudes about future use? Do you want to keep trying it? Do you want to stop? What people or events or situations might get you to smoke? What would get you to stop? What could I do to help you stop?

The Experimental Stage

Key points: Tell your children about the stages of smoking and warn them that in this stage they are beginning to discover all the things they like about tobacco. They are getting more deeply involved in smoking. It may have been easy to quit up until now, but the more they discover what they like about tobacco, the harder it will be to ever stop. Since much of the initial use of tobacco is with peers in social settings, you can discuss the context (where, when, and with whom the smoking takes place) in order to explore the question of social influence (see chapter six, under the heading "My Friends Have Nothing to Do with My Smoking"). Help your children evaluate if they have set any limits to their smoking. If not, explain that this means they are probably on the fast track toward regular smoking and eventual addiction.

Questions you will want answered over the course of time include:

- What do you like about smoking?
- Do you have any concerns about tobacco?
- If so, what are they?
- If not, why not?
- What are the types of situations in which you smoke? With which people? In what setting (home, parties, friends' houses, school, etc.)?
- Have you ever turned down cigarettes?
- If not, why not?
- If so, why?
- Are there situations in which you wouldn't smoke if offered tobacco?
- What's next? Do you plan to keep smoking? What people or events or situations will get you to smoke? What, if any, are your limits? What would it take to convince you to quit? What could I do to help you quit?

The Regular-Use Stage

Key points: With these smokers, you want to stress that they now enjoy smoking and are only one step removed from addiction. Ask them what they like about it. Point out that they are now seeking tobacco, smoking it regularly, and will eventually become addicted as their bodies develop tolerance for this drug. Explain the nature of addiction in a compelling way. For example: "As you know, now you are in control and chasing after the drug for a good feeling. But that will change. Eventually everything will be reversed. *The drug will control you.* You will need to always have tobacco and will feel uncomfortable, nervous, and edgy when you don't have it, or can't smoke it. This is the nature of addiction."

Sometimes it helps to explain to adolescents that the root of the word "addiction" means "slave to," and warn them that they may soon be a slave to tobacco. This is the last chance to stop without enormous pain and struggle.

By this point, some of the consequences of smoking may be evident. Discuss the financial cost of tobacco, the smell, the fact it is unappealing to many potential dating partners, and the trouble you can get into when caught smoking. Review the health consequences. Explore whether they have considered quitting and what it would take to quit.

Questions you will want answered over the course of time include:

- When did you start smoking regularly?
- How do you get cigarettes?
- What do you like about smoking?
- Why don't you smoke more often?
- Why don't you smoke less often?
- What are your concerns?
- Do you ever think about quitting?
- What's next? Are you committed to continuing to smoke? How committed? What would it take to quit? What do you think it would be like if you were addicted to tobacco? How could I help you quit?

When You Catch Children in the Act

I am sure some parents are reading this book after the fact— that is, after they have already discovered, or strongly suspected, that their children are using tobacco. You may have smelled tobacco on their clothing, their hair, or their breath. You may have smelled it in their room. You may have found a pack of cigarettes in their jacket (which perhaps they told you they were holding for a friend). Maybe you caught them in the act. Under these circumstances, I imagine you would be doubly upset (1) that your children are smoking and (2) that they were sneaking behind your back. Nevertheless, I remain consistent in my recommendations about dealing with tobacco. Don't panic. Take a moment to calm yourself. Understand the pressures that exist to try tobacco. If you haven't been talking about tobacco in your family, it is time to start now. Take a deep breath, and go back to basics. Tell your children that you are upset that they are using tobacco, and that they have not been honest with you. After that, you have the same challenge as all parents: to try to establish the sort of relationship in which your children can talk with you about anything, including tobacco. This is job one. When it is complete, you can lay the groundwork for progress by starting the exchange of information described in this chapter. We need to open the dialogue about tobacco.

Now we're ready to discuss the key roadblocks that sometimes prevent young people from understanding the full impact of the risks and harm from using tobacco.

▪ CHAPTER SIX ▪

Roadblocks
to Understanding

A sixteen-year-old girl who wants to be a psychologist when she grows up came to interview me about the profession. She surprised me by bringing along her boyfriend. In the course of our discussion, the girl complained that her boyfriend smokes. He replied, "I don't even know why I do it. I don't like the taste. I should stop."

"So, why don't you?" asked his girlfriend. (You could see she was destined to be a psychologist.)

"I really don't know," he answered. "It gets me in trouble. It costs a lot of money. I don't know why I do it."

"How much do you smoke?" I asked.

"Almost a pack a day," he answered.

"That's quite a bit," I said. "There must be something you like. What do you like best about it?"

His face lit up with an enormous smile, and he said: "*The buzz.*"

In discussions about tobacco, there are many roadblocks that prevent adolescents from objectively evaluating the extent of their involvement with this drug, as well as the full impact of the risks and harm from its use. One major roadblock, illustrated well in the above conversation, is that smokers often fail to understand how strongly

109

attached they are to tobacco. They are unaware of the depth of their need and desire for it, and of how much they fear losing it. Without this awareness, they may be confused, as this boy was, about why they keep smoking. Also, it may be easy for them to minimize their use, casually declaring that they can quit whenever they want, and naively believing that they will quit at some time in the near future. This chapter presents this and other roadblocks to awareness that prevent young people from fully understanding their tobacco use. It also suggests ways to address these roadblocks.

The Lure of Tobacco

As described earlier, most initial use of tobacco is done out of curiosity—perhaps for excitement, perhaps to rebel, perhaps for the sake of image. However, as people continue to smoke, they begin to develop a liking for the pharmacological effects of the drug. Some of them smoke, at least in part, because they simply enjoy the physical sensation. Many smokers quickly discover the mood-altering qualities and social benefits of the drug. They may enjoy the benefits without even realizing what they are seeking and the extent to which they are driven by physical, social, and emotional needs. With the adolescent population, in particular, it is sometimes difficult to get them to understand both *why* they are smoking and *how important* smoking has become in their lives.

Over the years of working with adolescents, I have learned not to ask the question "Why do you use tobacco?" The answer is almost always "Because I like it or because it feels good." (Why are you asking, you idiot?) My suggestion is that instead of asking your children why they smoke, ask them what they *like* about tobacco. Some adolescents can give simple answers: "It calms me down. It makes me relax. It's something to do when I'm bored. It's a cool activity with friends."

If your adolescent children have trouble identifying what they like, an excellent way to help them pin it down is with what I call "directed questions and labeling." Ask your children about recent times when they smoked: "Where were you? Who were you with? What were you feeling when you lit up? What did you feel as you smoked? What did you feel after you smoked?" Here's what sixteen-year-old Jody said: "I was with Emily. I was feeling really angry that Joshua didn't come to my house when he said he was going to come. I wanted to 'chill.' So we smoked. I think we both relaxed when we smoked and felt much better. After a cigarette or two, I was still mad at Joshua, but it didn't bother me as much."

I said: "Okay, let me see if I've got it right. You were with Emily, feeling angry and tense when you lit up. When you smoked, you relaxed and were less bothered by your anger. It sounds as though the cigarettes helped you cope with your tension and anger. Smoking kind of calmed you down. Maybe it was a social thing, too. Did Emily smoke with you?"

"Yes she did," Jody said. "It's what we do when we're upset."

"Oh," I said, "so it was kind of a social thing. And it calmed you down."

This type of feedback helps young people understand that they are using tobacco to meet their needs. It may sound as though it justifies smoking. Actually it serves as a warning that what may seem like a "feel-good" activity is actually more of a crutch. People recognize that they're using the drug for a purpose. To the extent that they lack other ways to meet their personal needs without tobacco, they have a high drug-neediness quotient (DNQ), which would put them at risk for addiction.

Jody was a regular smoker—smoking mainly in social situations—but not yet addicted. I decided to put her on alert: "Sounds like you *really* like tobacco. But, it's almost like a crutch for you. And that's kind of a red flag—a warning sign that you should think twice about continuing. I think you better be careful or you're going to start to depend on tobacco."

As I listened carefully to Jody, her attraction to tobacco was apparent. To really tap a person's attitude about tobacco, it's not enough simply to identify the purpose for which a drug is used. To fully understand the lure of tobacco, it's important to grasp the extent of the attraction.

A Secret Love Affair

In working with smokers, I sometimes ask them to make a list of both what they like about tobacco and what concerns them about this drug. However, a list does not always capture the depth of feelings. For example, on a list they might say that tobacco "calms me down." Given a chance to expand, they might add something such as this: "Tobacco is my friend. I always keep it close because it calms my nerves and settles me down whenever I'm tense. It's predictable. I can depend on it. It's there for me when I need it."

By the same token, a list of concerns about tobacco might say that "it's addictive, causes cancer, and causes heart disease." Given an opportunity to expand, they might say:

"It's a killer and it stalks me. I can't get away from it."

I like to ask teenagers to think about their "relationship" with tobacco. This helps them understand the attachment they have to this drug, how hard it might be to "break up," and the fears they may have about losing it. At the same time, it can reveal their resentment about the harmfulness of the drug and about the hold it has over them. I developed a simple exercise to tap into these feelings. In this exercise, you ask smokers to write a letter to tobacco—as if it were a person. Explain that this can be a thank-you letter for all that tobacco has given them, a love letter, or a letter expressing mixed emotions. Regardless, it should be a letter about the smoker's relationship with this drug.

In giving directions about writing this letter, encourage smokers to take their time and to write in some detail. Here is an actual letter written by a teen.

> *Dear Cigarettes,*
>
> *You are the worst thing that ever happened to me. You taste good but you hurt me. You keep me company when I am lonely. You have always been there for me when I needed you—at times of pain, anger, and stress. You are there to calm my nerves. You are there for me when I'm bored or happy. I depend on you. I trust you can help me. It is comforting to hold you in my hands and put you to my lips. You help me in times of need, but you hurt me. Why must you hurt me whenever you help? I want to break from you, but I never will. Who cares about all those people who call you bad names. I can trust you, and I'll be there for you with my lighter.*
>
> *Love,*
> *A Frequent Smoker*

You can see how a letter like this exposes the emotions attached to tobacco—and reveals some of the internal conflict about smoking. It provides much grist for discussion. It also, in some cases, reveals what I call a "hidden love affair." Adolescents who do this exercise often discover how very attached they are to tobacco. In turn, it causes them to challenge certain assumptions they may hold, such as "I just smoke a little" and "I could easily quit (if I wanted to)." The letter to tobacco also may increase their awareness of the potential harm from their smoking; make them realize what significant measures they must take to break loose of their habits; and inspire them to continue to develop healthier, drug-free ways of life.

I first thought about this exercise while reading the book *No If, Ands, or Butts: A Smoker's Guide to Kicking the Habit.* Julie Waltz, the author, spoke of tobacco as an "all-purpose tool." For smokers, she said, it is easier to use cigarettes to cope with emotions than to do just about anything else. She spoke of the way that smokers see themselves as "soothed, comforted, quieted, distracted, stimulated, kept company, occupied and pleasured by cigarettes." It sounded like a relationship to me, even if it is only a "secret affair."

The Rationalization Game

In discussing their use of tobacco, young people make certain statements that reflect a lack of understanding of the addiction process. These statements sometimes reveal what they actually think about their use of tobacco, and other times represent a defense against what they perceive as pressure to quit smoking. Whatever the reason, these statements interfere with an objective evaluation of tobacco use. Below I have selected some of the most prominent rationalizations and provided ideas about how to respond to them. As always with the exchange-of-information model, it's important to be respectful and supportive, even when challenging or disagreeing with something your sons or daughters might have said.

"It's No Big Deal; I Just Smoke a Little"

Many beginning smokers are naive about addiction. They rightfully defend their initial use of tobacco as "just trying it" or mere dabbling. They say: "I'm not really a smoker. I just smoke once in a while, just when it's around. I don't go looking for it. I'm not hooked. I could stop whenever I want."

You could respond with the following: "I understand what you're saying. I can see that you're only in the early stages of tobacco use. I bet you could stop if you wanted, just as you have said. You know, I wish you would make exactly that choice. One of the things I know about tobacco is that it is extraordinarily addictive. Everyone who smokes (or chews) tobacco starts as you have started. No one expects to get addicted to it. Addiction really sneaks up on people."

Then I would say, "I want to tell you more about addiction," and start with something such as one of the following three paragraphs, depending on which stage of smoking your child has reached.

For children in the trying stage: "First, people think about using tobacco. Then some of them try it two or three times, just as you have. Unless they stop at this point, they next begin experimenting with it—a little here and a little there, but only when it is available or the situation is right. They still think that they're safe because they smoke just a little. But then they begin to smoke more. They get comfortable with tobacco, start to like it, become regular smokers, and eventually become addicted. Until they were addicted, they could have easily stopped if they made up their mind to quit. But they never made that decision. Most addicted smokers remember looking back to earlier days when they said that they were smoking 'just a little' and would never get hooked. But they were wrong. They had no clue. Even though you've just begun smoking, I urge you to think twice about going any further."

For children in the experimenting stage: "First, people think about using tobacco. Then some of them try it. Unless they stop at this point, next they begin experimenting with tobacco, as you've been doing—a little here and a little there, only when tobacco just happens to be available. You probably think that you're safe because you just smoke a little. But if you don't quit now, the next step is smoking more often and in more and more different situations. When people do this, they begin to feel comfortable with tobacco and like its effects. Gradually they become regular smokers, without even realizing it. Eventually they become addicted. Until they were addicted, they could have easily stopped if they made up their mind to quit. But they never made that decision. Most addicted smokers remember looking back to earlier days when they said that they were smoking 'just a little' and would never get hooked. But they were wrong. They had no clue. Even though you just smoke a little right now, I urge you to think twice about what you're doing and where it can lead."

For children in the regular-use stage: "First, people think about using tobacco. Then some of them try it two or three times, then some begin more serious experimentation. Unless they stop before this point, the next stage is regular use—which is what you're doing—smoking more often and in more situations. In the past you haven't been looking for tobacco. But if you think about it now, you sometimes seek it. Your use isn't as light as it used to be. As your body develops tolerance for tobacco, you'll need more of it for the same effect, unless you put an end to this. You'll eventually become addicted. Do you really think that you smoke just a little, and it's no big deal? I disagree. The next stage is addiction. You know, most addicted smokers remember looking back to earlier days when they said that they were smoking 'just a little' and would never get hooked. But they were wrong. They had no clue."

Regardless of stage, if smokers persist in asserting that they "just smoke a little," I would ask them to establish criteria for what constitutes more than a little, and what would be the first possible indication that they were drifting in that direction. This would at least represent a personal indicator, by their own definition, of danger ahead.

"I'll Quit Later"

Many youth who see themselves as dabbling with tobacco say that their smoking will end in the near future, often presuming they will not get addicted. They say, "I'll quit later." I usually ask them, "If you see tobacco as something you want to quit, why will you quit later and not now?" One response is that tobacco only causes health harm after many years of smoking. But this is not true. Smokers need to understand the health consequences of smoking discussed in chapter two. You can help your children understand that every cigarette is bad for their health—right now.

I would ask, "If you don't quit now, what makes you think you can stop later? Won't your body be more accustomed to tobacco and possibly addicted to it in the future?"

Finally, in responding to "I just smoke a little," I concur with the Surgeon General's Report, which stated that "young people should be made aware of the highly addictive nature of nicotine and its ability to overwhelm future good expectations." One way to make children aware of this is by telling them about the results of a survey in which researchers asked high school seniors who smoked if they thought they would still be smoking in five years. Their predictions were way off the mark. Many more of them smoked than thought would be smoking in five years, *and* they were smoking many more cigarettes than they had predicted. Of the seniors who smoked a pack a day or more, 87 percent were still smoking five to six years later. Of those who smoked half a pack a day, 81 percent still smoked, and the majority of them increased their rate of smoking. Of those who smoked one to five cigarettes per day, 70 percent of them smoked five years later, most of them increasing their rate of use. Even among those who smoked the least (less than one cigarette per day), 42 percent continued smoking five to six years later *and* two-thirds of these had increased their rate of smoking. *Let your children know that people who predict they will quit in the future are on shaky ground.* The safest course of action is to quit now. Tobacco is enormously addictive.

"You Can't Make Me Quit; It's My Choice"

Remember that the tone of the exchange of information is crucial. It is important *not* to lock horns with adolescent children. We want to conduct a respectful discussion, in a calm tone, in order to advance their thinking and reduce defensiveness. Also, we do not want to become an authority figure against which our children rebel—one factor that commonly motivates tobacco use in the first place is the desire of young people to assert their independence, or sometimes, to defy parental wishes or rules. Bearing this in mind, I would be inclined to agree with adolescents who say, "You can't stop me."

"You're right. Ultimately this is your decision. I can't police you all the time. You can get cigarettes and smoke when I'm not around.

"Right now I'm just trying to have a discussion because I love you and want to express my point of view and listen to yours. I love you too much to remain silent on this important health issue. In the end, however, it's going to be your choice, just as you say."

The idea of "I'm free" and "no one can stop me" from smoking has been referred to as "foolish freedom." It means that a person is declaring him or herself free—free to engage in a health-compromising behavior. What freedom! Perhaps with your children you can discuss healthier ways that they could invent to declare their independence and freedom from external restraints.

"I Could Quit Right Now (If I Wanted To)"

Smokers in the early stages of tobacco use quite justifiably say they could quit right now if they wanted to. However, many addicted smokers say the same thing. People who make an assertion about ease of quitting need to take an objective look at their smoking habits, and consider how much they smoke; how often they smoke; whether they ever crave cigarettes; and whether their tolerance of nicotine has increased, as evidenced by an increase in the amount of tobacco consumed. Their track record on quitting is also a good indicator. You might ask: "Have you ever tried to quit? If so, why did you resume smoking again?" If they have never tried, then ask, "What makes you think it would be so easy to quit now?" Also, ask them to consider this question: "Have you ever tried to go a week without smoking?" If not, perhaps they can try this in order to assess the extent of their habit.

"My Friends Have Nothing to Do with My Smoking"

As discussed in chapter four, research evidence strongly supports the role of peer influence in smoking among teenagers. Many people think of peer influence in its most obvious form—when one child, or a group of children, calls another child a "chicken" and pressures him or her to smoke. This type of overt pressure does occur, especially with younger children. However, most peer pressure is the indirect/subtle type, in which all peers do the same thing, share the same experience, and quietly expect others to join in. Those who don't participate—in this case by not smoking (or chewing) tobacco—feel that they are on the "outside."

Despite the evidence that peer pressure is a strong influence, most adolescents will deny it. They will say, "I'm not following a crowd or anything. It's my own decision to smoke. It's part of the fun of being together and hanging out with each other."

Sometimes they come closer to recognizing peer pressure in statements such as these:

• "All the other kids are smoking."
• "I can't imagine being at a party and not smoking."
• "I can't imagine being with (best friend) and not smoking."

It seems that we need to help children understand that they are probably experiencing indirect/subtle peer pressure. Do we simply tell them so? You can try. Some adolescents are inspired to "go against the crowd" when they come to understand that they have been influenced or controlled by others. More often, however, young people do *not* want to hear that they are being swayed by peers. If you mention peer pressure, they get very defensive: "No, no. I smoke tobacco because I want to, not because I'm afraid of what other kids will think." Therefore, most often, it makes more sense to be subtle in addressing issues of peer pressure, and to avoid the "peer pressure" label. You could say something like this: "I can see that smoking is a big part of the fun you have with your friends and that it's hard to imagine being with them without sharing in this experience. I know you don't want to miss the action. And I know it's not much fun to be the only one not participating. But I still think it's a big mistake to smoke—even if you miss out on the fun with friends. *You* know the bad stuff about smoking. I don't need to repeat it."

If your teen says, "But everyone does it," you can refer to the data on prevalence and to the preference of teenagers to date nonsmokers cited on page 72.

Sometimes smoking is not so much influenced by peer pressure as it is by social anxiety. It can be stressful to socialize during adolescence, with hormones kicking in, a new interest in dating and sexuality, a new and perhaps shaky sense of identity, and a strong need for belonging. Young people often smoke simply to relax in a social setting. For example, they may be calmed by the physical effects of the tobacco or by the act of holding the cigarette, a social prop, in their hands. If this is the case with your child, I suggest reviewing chapter four and saying something such as the following: "Gee, it would be a real loss not to have a cigarette when you are at parties, or meeting new people, or want to just plain feel comfortable with friends. I gather you get a lot of comfort from smoking. But I still doubt that it's worth it. I know it feels good. But this is how people end up addicted. There are others way to make yourself feel comfortable. I can help you with this if you want. What do you think?"

"Tobacco Is the Least of My Problems"

When children say tobacco is the least of their problems, adults are tempted to get confrontational. We sometimes try to convince them that smoking is a serious health hazard. Adolescents usually know this already, although perhaps they are not as affected by the knowledge as we might wish. Unfortunately, crusades about the dangers of tobacco, in this context, generally generate the opposite of the desired effect. Teens tend to defend their smoking.

I recommend an entirely different and radical approach: Take the adolescent seriously!

"I am sorry to hear that you are so troubled."

"What are your big problems? What is it that upsets you so much?"

"What are you doing about it?"

"How can I help you?"

Then days or weeks *later*—after you have seriously addressed the issues that your children see as primary and after you have established yourself as a problem-solving partner— you can again bring up the tobacco issue. "I can see that these other problems are really important to you. And maybe it seems as though stopping your use of tobacco would add stress. But I still think it's important to consider the possibility of quitting."

Teens might complain that quitting tobacco would mean losing an effective way of coping with stress. That is why, of course, it is so important that we continue our efforts at teaching them healthy ways of coping. If you haven't already done this, you can offer to teach your children the deep breathing and muscle relaxation exercises presented in chapter three, and help them find other healthy ways to cope with stress.

"With All the Stress in My Life, This Is Not a Good Time to Quit"

This roadblock sounds like a cop-out because there may never be a *good time* to quit. Life is filled with stress. It will never disappear. So, you might be tempted to challenge smokers by asking them when, if ever, would be a good time. One problem, however, is that people might actually be experiencing periods of unusually high stress, and these probably are not the best times to quit using tobacco products. Another problem with this type of challenge is that it can get argumentative. I believe it is preferable to "join" with a smoker who complains of stress, as in the following, and then to slowly work your way toward the idea of establishing a time to quit smoking.

"What is the stress that stands in the way of quitting tobacco? What can you do about the stress? How could I help you with it? How does tobacco help you? Do you know any healthier coping strategies that maybe you could use to deal with this stress? Would you be interested in learning healthier ways?"

After these questions are addressed, you can then redirect attention toward establishing a time to quit using tobacco.

"We All Have to Die Sometime"

Smokers who are aware of the self-destructive nature of smoking may resort to the thinking pattern known as "cut-off." This allows them rapidly to eliminate consideration of the harm from their smoking by resorting to a simple phrase such as "I don't care" or a rationalization such as "We all have to die sometime." I am inclined to respond by saying something such as this: "I believe that you don't *want* to care. But I don't believe, in your heart of hearts, that you don't care. I imagine you care a lot. I think it is hard to accept sometimes that you are doing something that is bad for you. So you try to cut off this awareness. But you know as well as I do that using tobacco is a terrible habit. I am concerned about it and about your health. I hope you will think twice about it, too."

Fear of Failure

Sometimes smokers are well aware of the dangers of tobacco but won't commit to quitting because of fear they will fail. Many of them have already failed at previous attempts to quit. I believe that the best response to the fear of failure is to say, "Quitting takes practice." We should tell adolescents that people often make two, or three, or more attempts at quitting before they finally succeed. People who want to quit should never give up. They can learn from previous attempts and seek advice, such as that offered in chapters seven and eight, which will increase their odds for success.

As you have seen, the exchange-of-information model is a way to have a reasonable, disciplined discussion of important emotional issues. It is inherently calm, deliberate, and thorough. It requires give-and-take dialogue. Parents and children need to ask each other questions to understand one another's point of view. You can't rush. You can't pressure. Yet tobacco is an addictive drug, and you do need to reach some understanding. After a thorough discussion, make sure you understand your child's point of view. Ask your child if he or she understands yours, or needs more clarification. If everything checks out, you are ready for a discussion of tobacco decisions—to use, to not use, or to quit—the topic of the next chapter.

CHAPTER SEVEN

Decisions and Agreements about Tobacco

Melissa's parents were understandably alarmed that their fourteen-year-old daughter was smoking ten to fifteen cigarettes per day. Taking my advice, they initiated an exchange of information about tobacco, which they felt had been successful.

When I asked Melissa how it went, she said, "Okay, I guess."

When I asked how it ended, she said, "I *told* them I was going to quit." The emphasis was clearly on the "told" part, not the quitting. So I asked, "Are you *really* going to quit?"

"No, no," she said, "but it was the only way to get them off my back."

Melissa then admitted that the discussion didn't go well. "They pretended to be reasonable, but kept hammering away at me about smoking. When I started to say what I liked about smoking, they tried to argue me down. When I *stupidly* admitted I was worried about my cough, they named three million diseases I could get from tobacco. It was like they backed me into a corner. I got sick of it. I got sick of them. I got sick of the whole thing. So I told them what they wanted to hear—that I was quitting. And that ended it."

Most parents know the dangers of tobacco and would like their children to quit smoking immediately. But as this case shows, parents can be overly eager and push too hard too soon. The *rush* for a commitment to quit usually back-fires—with lies as it did in Melissa's family, or with rebellion. To avoid these pitfalls, we need to give adolescents some space to think for themselves. We must make it safe for them to say what they *really* think and feel, even if they don't choose abstinence. We should also give kids who smoke a chance to quit of their own free will before we consider the possibility of applying pressure.

The Final Phase

The last part of the exchange of information is about making agreements and decisions. First, parents need to find out what their children have concluded—of their own accord. Parents can begin by saying: "What are *your* conclusions? What do you want to do about tobacco?" Or teens can get the ball rolling with a question of their own: "Well, we've talked, so what's the deal now?"

My response to this question would be:

"You know what I think? I think tobacco is a dangerous and addictive drug. I very much wish you would decide not to use it. But I'd like to know what *you* think and what *you* want to do. I hope you feel you can tell me the truth. And, you *don't* have to tell me that you won't smoke (or, that you're going to quit). I want to hear the truth. If we disagree, we'll just have to face our differences."

Most nonsmokers will say that they want to continue to abstain. Some may not be certain about future plans. With these kids, you can agree to keep the discussion alive, so that, hope-fully, they will choose to remain tobacco-free. Some nonsmokers may say they plan to start smoking. This could be a test of your reaction—don't panic. Or it may be a serious considera-tion. If it is, I recommend you make an effort to understand your child's motivation to smoke, show some understanding of it, and then urge that he or she reconsider. If the desire to smoke persists, you could either forbid smoking (which may work but also could stimulate defiance) or reluctantly tolerate it. These two options are discussed later in this chapter. If your children do break the barrier and start smoking, then they move into the category of "smokers" discussed below.

When adolescents who smoke discuss their conclusions about future behavior, they may start with one of four positions:

- I'm not sure what I want to do.
- I want to quit, but I'm not ready.
- I want to quit.
- I want to keep on smoking.

The rest of this chapter is about responding to these positions.

The Many Meanings of "I Want to Quit"

A sixteen-year-old boy named Sean told me that he wanted to stop smoking. At the moment he said this, I think he meant it. But it appeared to me that this was more of a passing thought than a sincere commitment. So, I asked, "What would you do if I put a pack of cigarettes and a lighter on the table, right now, right here in front of you?"

Sean answered without hesitation: "Oh, I'd smoke them for sure."

Then he realized what he was saying and smiled, slightly embarrassed. As we continued to talk, it became clear that he wasn't faking it. He was really confused. He hadn't considered the enormous difference between having a passing desire to quit and being firmly committed to it. He needed to figure out exactly where he stood.

As the discussion continued, I could see that Sean was ambivalent about tobacco. He still liked smoking—any reminder of the pleasures of tobacco sparked his desire to smoke. But when he was being rational about it—talking to an adult, away from friends, and not exposed to other reminders of smoking—he had some very serious health concerns, and a real desire to quit. I reassured Sean that mixed feelings of this sort are quite normal and offered to help strengthen the healthy "wanting to quit" side. At this point, Sean recognized his position: firmly perched, sitting on the fence between smoking and quitting.

As you can see, the desire to stop smoking—as expressed in the statement "I want to quit"—can mean different things to different people. It can be anything from a passing thought, to a serious consideration, to a firm goal. This is an important distinction. If your children say that they want to quit, you can help them determine where they stand by asking them to identify which of the following statements best describes their thinking:

- *Firmly committed:* I will not smoke tobacco under any circumstances. I am ready to firmly resist the urge, even when I am tempted.
- *I'm not sure:* I have mixed feelings about tobacco. I want to quit, but I also want to keep smoking. I go back and forth between the two positions.
- *I'm not ready:* I want to quit. I know that would be best. I made up my mind. But I'm not yet ready to do it.

Smokers need to understand that to successfully break the tobacco habit, they must be *firmly committed to quitting.* Anything less leads to failure. Sometimes people try to quit without such a commitment, perhaps actually stop for a short period of time, but eventually relapse when the "right" situations arise. These relapses make them feel like a "fail-ure," strengthen their fear that they could never overcome their tobacco habit, and ultimately reinforce a sense of pow-erlessness over this drug.

People who are "not sure" or "not ready" should be cautioned about declaring their intent to quit. They can be encouraged to consider other, less demanding options, such as cutting back on the amount smoked or stopping for a short period of time. (These are discussed in more detail later in this chapter.) Meanwhile, they need to keep think-ing about the issue of quitting. Those who are "not sure" will need to resolve their uncertainties and ambivalence. Those who are "not yet ready" to quit will need to identify and overcome the obstacles that prevent them from com-mitting to action.

How to Respond to "I'm Not Sure"

Adolescents in the "I'm not sure" category are of two minds about smoking. They (1) want to continue and (2) have doubts about it. In discussions, it's important to give them credit for having these doubts. As a first step in negotiation, you can try to tip the balance toward quitting by *urging* a pro-health choice. You want to sway their thinking, if possi-ble, without starting a power struggle. For example: "I see you have mixed feelings about smoking. You like it, but also think it's bad for you. As you know, I think tobacco is very dangerous. I'm glad that you've been thinking about the dangers, too. *I want to ask you to quit smoking.* I know it means sacrificing something you like. It may not be clear to you now, but I'm certain, if you quit, someday you'll be very glad you did. If you agree to quit, I'll help you succeed at it. If you want to start by just cutting back, I'll help you with that, or any other small, first steps you might want to take."

Then I suggest parents back off, pause, and give their kids a little time for reflection. Strong parental *requests* of this kind can be effective, especially when there is a strong parent-child bond.

If despite your urging your children still want to smoke, there are three viable and very different alternatives. The best choice depends on a number of factors. One option is to request a one- or two-week *moratorium* on smoking while your kids think more about their decisions. After the moratorium, the discussion resumes. This approach buys time for additional thought and provides a "break" from tobacco. If children will not or cannot refrain from smoking, this lets them see how deeply involved they are with this drug. A second option, discussed below, is to *reluctantly tolerate* both the continued uncertainty about tobacco and its continued use. A third option is to *apply increased pressure* to try to make your children quit, starting with your insistence that they stop. If you choose this option, I suggest moderating it with a statement such as this: "I don't like setting rules I know you won't like. But I love you too much to sit on the sidelines while you continue to smoke. You really must stop. It's a rule in this family. Obviously at some point in your life it'll be your decision alone. You won't have to follow my rules. Meanwhile, I trust you'll obey me about tobacco."

Using pressure will work with some youth but backfire with others. It's more likely to work with younger adolescents. Its effectiveness is also influenced by the level of commitment to smoking, the strength of the smoking habit, the extent to which the child tends to submit to authority, and the quality of the parent-child relationship. The risk, however, is that pressure might cause some teens to rebel and become even more determined to smoke. Another risk is that they will feel threatened and "go underground." That is, they'll tell you they are quitting, but be sneaky and keep smoking. You don't want to set a rule you can't enforce, or one that could inadvertently increase the desire to use tobacco, or possibly erode trust and end the dialogue.

I recently asked a teenage girl, a high school junior in a gifted program, if she could talk openly about personal matters with her mother and stepfather. She told me she could, "most of the time." I asked about the times when she could *not* talk personally. She said, "Well, there are certain things I do that I know they wouldn't like. I *never* tell them about those things." In other words, she was open and honest as long as her parents approved of her behavior, but sneaky about the rest. "They have no clue," she said, "that I smoke cigarettes. They caught me once, threw a fit, and made me promise that I'd never smoke again. So I promised. What else could I do?"

You know your own children best, and can determine whether you think a rule will work. If you use one, your intuition is an excellent resource in trying to determine whether the rule is being followed or you are being conned. When a rule is broken, there should be consequences. However, the risk with a hard line is that adolescents will get sneakier or more defiant.

If older adolescents plan to continue smoking despite your urging, I would be inclined to recommend the strategy of *reluctant tolerance*. With this, you express disappointment about their choice to smoke, but avoid a power struggle. It's then important to follow through with ongoing discussions and to establish certain rules. I would say something like this: "I realize I can't stop you from using tobacco. So I will tolerate it. But I'm your parent and I love you very much. I want to keep this discussion going, and will keep talking about tobacco from time to time. I haven't given up hope that you'll recognize how harmful this habit is, and that you might one day decide to quit. In the meantime there are some rules that must be respected. There can be no smoking in our home, in the family car, and while with the family. This is to protect our right to a smoke-free environment, uncluttered of ashtrays and cigarette butts, and free of the smell of tobacco."

In your discussions, it's important to bring up the topic of personal limits. Adolescents who reject parental guidance and parental rules are presumably taking responsibility for their own choices. This raises the question of where *they* stand on smoking. What are their self-imposed limits? Parents can ask: "How much do you intend to allow yourself to smoke? What are the limits, if any, you have set for yourself?"

If smokers set and abide by limits, it can prevent deeper involvement with tobacco. If they cannot abide by limits, they may see that their tobacco use is out of control, which could precipitate a change of heart. If they choose to set no limits at all, you can point out that *unlimited* use of tobacco is likely to result in addiction.

From time to time you'll want to check with your kids on what they're thinking about tobacco, taking another look at what they like and what, if anything, concerns them about it. One method of increasing awareness of the dangers is to discuss and keep a record of your child's movement through the stages of tobacco use (trying, experimenting, regular use, addiction). You can also chart the amount of tobacco consumed over time. Adolescent smokers will probably see that their use increases as you monitor it together. This can help them recognize that they are on a dangerous course.

How to Respond to "I Want to Quit, But I'm Not Ready"

Some smokers are quite clear that they should stop smoking. They know it's harmful and would like to quit, but simply are not ready to take the plunge. Most often smokers are stuck because they're addicted or because they're getting something good from tobacco that they are reluctant to give up. They need a little extra motivation. Because they are not ready to quit, they sometimes mistakenly see themselves as *wanting to smoke.* However, when carefully questioned, they realize this is not so. They would like to quit but have been unable to follow through. Many of them are down on themselves about this. To cast a more positive spin on their dilemma, we can help them see themselves as *preparing for action.*

People in this category are probably aware of the dangers and consequences of smoking. That's why they want to quit. Being reminded of the health hazards might simply add to their frustration. One strategy that sometimes inspires action is to help not-ready-to-quit smokers focus on the good things that will happen when they become tobacco-free. You can tell them about the benefits of quitting:

- Within the first day, the carbon monoxide level in their blood returns to normal and their heart rate slows.
- Within a few days, the mucus in their airways breaks up and clears out of their lungs.
- Within a few weeks, circulation improves and they'll breathe better; they'll be able to smell better; food will taste better.
- Within a year, their risk of lung cancer begins to decrease.

No more wheezing, coughing, and hacking. Hands and teeth will no longer be stained yellow. They'll feel better when they exercise. They'll smell good. They'll save money. They'll never have to worry about finding an ashtray. They won't be a slave to this drug.

Another obstacle to a commitment to quitting is that smokers find it difficult to let go of the social and emotional benefits of tobacco. They need help seeing that they can manage their lives without tobacco.

I worked with a teenage boy who said he wanted to quit, but realized that he smoked tobacco to calm himself down. He said he hadn't been able to quit because he *needs* cigarettes to cope with stress. I reassured him that he could learn to cope in other ways, and then taught him a very simple deep-breathing exercise (see chapter three). That's all it took for him to quit. He just needed to believe that there was something he could do about stress.

Addicted smokers often fall in the "not ready" category. Many of them realize how hard it'll be to quit and lack confidence in their ability to succeed. Sometimes this is because they don't know how to quit. They need help with the specifics, which can be found in chapter eight.

Another way to boost the confidence of smokers about their ability to quit is to suggest that they start with smaller steps, such as reducing the amount they smoke or breaking the pattern of their smoking. You could encourage them with a statement such as this: "Tobacco is a very tough habit to break. I know you want to quit. Maybe you're not ready to quit *completely* right now. That's okay, but you can start by taking small, first steps that will move you in the right direction."

Small steps give people an opportunity to experience some success and provide a context for an ongoing discussion, and for reinforcing the idea of ultimately quitting.

Taking Small Steps

One small step your child could take is just a trial at stopping—perhaps for a limited time. Another small step is to gradually reduce the amount of tobacco used. This is good preparation for eventually quitting. A third small step is to keep using tobacco, but to break the usual pattern of consumption. For example: someone who usually smokes first thing in the morning would refrain for at least fifteen minutes after waking up; someone who usually smokes while on the telephone would abstain until after hanging up. Breaking the pattern begins to weaken the habit and makes it easier to eventually quit. A fourth small step is to make lifestyle changes that lay the groundwork for quitting. For example, a person could begin a vigorous program of physical activity, which is a way of life ultimately incompatible with smoking. It would reinforce both the need and desire to quit. Another example of a lifestyle change is to start eating a healthier diet. This mitigates against weight gain if the decision to quit is eventually made. Lifestyle changes empower people to feel they can control their lives and ultimately break their tobacco habit.

Small-step strategies, such as those described above, can be combined for added effectiveness. Singly or in combinations, they give people a chance to prepare for the bigger commitment of quitting.

Recognizing the Patterns and Breaking Them

Success in breaking the pattern of tobacco consumption—changing when and where smoking occurs—requires planning. Smokers first must identify the times, places, and situations in which they habitually smoke. They can begin by simply thinking about it, and making a list off the top of their heads. They'll come up with items such as these: after meals, first thing in the morning, while driving, while on the phone, whenever I hang out with (particular friend), at parties, whenever I'm stressed, when I'm bored, to reward myself after working hard, etc. An excellent way to fill out that picture is by keeping a chart of all the times they smoke during a week. The chart would have five columns:

Time	Place	Who I was with	What I was thinking	What I was feeling

One difficulty in keeping charts is that people often smoke by habit, without conscious awareness. They find themselves puffing on a cigarette without even realizing that they had decided to light one up—they don't know what prompted the use. So I suggest an old trick: smokers can keep their packs of cigarettes wrapped in notebook paper, with a rubber band running top to bottom, and a second one side to side, across the pack. This arrangement prevents them from lighting up without being aware of it. They might unconsciously reach for their cigarettes in a pocket or purse—but would become aware of what they are doing as they unwrap the pack from the notebook paper. This trick helps them chart their tobacco use and become aware of their smoking patterns—when they smoke, with whom, where, and in response to which feelings and which thoughts.

Once the patterns are clear and the "triggers" for smoking have been identified, smokers can continue to smoke at previous levels if they wish, but will not allow themselves to smoke in response to the usual triggers—at the usual times, places, or situations. This type of switching actually weakens the habit. It also allows smokers to see that urges to smoke come in waves—which can be weathered until they pass.

How to Respond to "I Want to Quit"

When your adolescent children are firmly committed to quitting, I suggest you enthusiastically praise their decision and ask how you could be helpful. Some youth want to do it all on their own. You shouldn't impose yourself, but could mention that quitting is sometimes very difficult and urge that they consider accepting your support. If your children decline your offer, I suggest simply asking them about their quit date, showing them chapter eight of this book, and then leaving them alone. Later you can ask about their progress.

How to Respond to "I Want to Keep on Smoking"

Falling in the category of adolescents who intend to keep smoking are (1) those who initially said they were going to keep doing it and (2) those who considered quitting, but never followed through.

As discussed earlier, I would try to get a reversal by asking your children to quit at your request. If that doesn't work, I would consider the possibility of insisting on it, also as discussed earlier.

Assuming you have used all your power in constructive ways to try to swing their decision toward quitting, and you believe that further insistence might possibly backfire, there is little left but to reluctantly tolerate the behavior. The advantage of such tolerance is that it avoids a power struggle and leaves the channels of communication open. While you are conceding that smoking will continue, I would make it clear that you'll keep bringing up the subject again because you consider it a serious health matter. I would also establish certain limits and rules about not smoking at home or with the family.

As your discussions about tobacco continue, you will want to identify and target the underlying factors that motivate or maintain your child's smoking. Does your child:

1. underestimate the harm?
2. see dangers as too far off in the distant future?
3. lack an understanding of the addiction process and think he or she can "get away with it"?
4. feel immune to the dangers, as in "It won't happen to me"?
5. have strong emotional needs that drive the use?
6. have strong peer-approval needs that drive the use?
7. feel that he or she could not successfully break the tobacco habit?

Most children smoke for several of the above reasons. If it is any of the first four, you can address the problem with drug education, referring to chapters one and two.

If it is reasons five and six, it is a question of drug neediness, and you'll want to follow basic good parenting practices aimed at empowering your children to meet their social and emotional needs without tobacco. The more you teach the life skills discussed in chapters three and four—such as how to handle stress, how to manage anger, how to have a good recreational life, and how to socialize comfortably with peers—the lower your children's drug-neediness quotient. This puts them in a position where they, themselves, might eventually choose to give up tobacco because they don't feel the social or emotional *need* for it anymore.

If your children smoke because they feel unable to break the tobacco habit (reason seven on the list), you can work with them on understanding the process of overcoming serious habits, and help them feel more powerful and optimistic about success. They can begin by taking small steps, as discussed in this chapter. Other ways to beat tobacco addiction are discussed in the following chapter.

More about the Magic of Reluctant Tolerance

During the final phase of the exchange-of-information process, the hope of health-conscious parents is certainly that their children will choose to be tobacco-free. Many of them will make this choice. Sadly, some will choose to continue smoking.

I don't want to express undue optimism about the sad reality of teenagers committed to smoking. However, on numerous occasions I have seen an important shift when parents use the strategy of reluctant tolerance. When they recognize that they cannot control the behavior of their teenage children and stop trying to police them, the response is sometimes paradoxical. Suddenly, children are no longer defensively fighting off their parents while defending their tobacco habits. When they stop resisting parental pressure, they are left to think for themselves. I remember one boy who said to me: "When my parents finally stopped bugging me about tobacco, I was kind of shocked. And I wasn't so sure it was such a good idea to smoke." This is what we are striving to attain, regardless of strategy: we want to tap our children's best judgment about their own health and welfare.

Ultimately we hope all smokers can be motivated to quit. Once they finally make this decision, they still face the difficult task of following through with it, which is the topic of the next chapter.

CHAPTER EIGHT

Helping Your Child Quit

Tobacco addiction has been called the most difficult addiction to break, right up there with heroin and cocaine. Beating the habit is an enormous challenge, as Jared, a fifteen-year-old pack-a-day smoker discovered: "I was really surprised. I kept telling people I could quit whenever I wanted. So when I decided to quit, I thought it would be easy. I was okay the first day. It wasn't as easy as I thought—but I was still confident. The next day I was hanging with my friends at the mall and they were all smoking, and I started thinking I wanted to smoke too. I held off for a while. Then I said, 'Oh, why not?' Next thing I knew—there was a lit cigarette in my mouth. I really blew it."

This disappointed teen has plenty of company. Each year, twenty million people try to quit smoking and only three percent have long-term success. Even among individuals who have lost a lung because of cancer or endured major cardiovascular surgery, only about 50 percent maintain abstinence for more than a few weeks. It's not any better for adolescents. Most teens who smoke a pack a day are addicted to nicotine and report that they want to quit, but are unable to do so. They experience relapse rates and withdrawal symptoms similar to those reported by adults.

Commitment to Quitting

Although more than 70 percent of addicted smokers would like to quit, there's a big difference between wanting something and actually doing it. Quitting requires enormous willpower over a prolonged period of time. People who quit must consistently resist urges to smoke, sometimes very strong ones—or they will relapse. I like to make the distinction between *stopping*, which means giving up tobacco for a short, or indefinite, period of time, and *quitting*, which means giving it up permanently. If people aren't committed to a total effort at resisting their urges over the long haul, they should be encouraged to either increase their expectations, or to think of themselves as stopping. We want to maximize success. Successful episodes of stopping are preferable to failures at quitting. When people relapse from attempts to quit, they are likely to feel defeated: "I can't ever beat this habit. I said I was going to quit and I've failed." It would be better if they set limited goals and felt empowered by episodes of success: "I said I was going to stop. I stopped for a while. That was a success. Next time I'll stop longer. Someday I will quit for good."

One of the problems with teen smoking is that we sometimes jump the gun in demanding tobacco cessation. When we catch them smoking, or learn that they are smoking, there is a tendency to punish them and insist they stop immediately. We assume they are ready and willing to quit because we have demanded it. If we provide help, it is usually in tobacco cessation—teaching them how to quit. However, we skip the important stages of contemplation, preparation, and decision making that always precede action. Similarly, when students are caught smoking in schools, tobacco-cessation classes are sometimes offered as an alternative to suspension. In these classes, young people are taught the very best principles of *how* to quit, but they have not even decided that they *want* to quit. It's a waste of time and a setup for failure. We should start with help on making the decision, before teaching anything about the behavior. For this, I refer you to the three previous chapters.

What You Can Do to Help

Social support and encouragement have been shown to increase the success rate of people quitting tobacco. However, adolescents tend to be ambivalent about getting help and support from their parents. On one hand, they proclaim their independence. On the other hand, they still feel the tug of dependency. They want our help, but also push us away. To navigate these troubled waters, we must carefully avoid making judgments and moralistic statements about tobacco use. Tobacco should be considered a health issue ("It's bad for you"), not a question of morality ("You are behaving badly"). Also, we should recognize that teens who have decided to quit do not need further information about the health hazards. The decision has already been made. They need support. I suggest offering it in gentle ways, with statements such as: "I want to 'be there' for you. What can I do to back up your efforts to quit? How can I help?"

As I wrote in the previous chapter, if your children don't want your help, inquire about their quit date, and back off. You might offer them access to professional care or simply an opportunity to read this chapter. If, however, they accept your help, there's much that can be done to lend emotional support and to prepare them for success.

Addicted smokers want your enthusiastic endorsement of the wisdom of what they're doing, your belief in their ability to succeed, and your understanding of how hard it is to overcome this addiction. You can make yourself available when they want problem-solving assistance, or want to talk about their feelings, or need help resisting an urge to smoke. During the withdrawal period, you can be more flexible and tolerant of some of the moodiness that may occur, and try extra hard to reduce stress at home. As the weeks and months pass, you can and should continue to praise their effort and to provide emotional support.

The "don'ts" of helping adolescents quit are also important. You shouldn't lecture or use scare tactics. You shouldn't nag, put down, or confront in hostile ways. I strongly advise against hiding ashtrays, throwing out cigarettes, or doing anything that could be perceived as taking over and challenging the autonomy of your adolescent child.

Adopting the Right Perspective

Some young smokers seriously underestimate the effort required to quit. So that they can prepare adequately, they need to know that they'll be facing a strong challenge to their will, determination, and capacity to cope. Most people do *not* succeed in quitting on their first attempt. But even as we speak of the difficulty of the challenge, we should also encourage young people to believe that they can succeed, even on their first attempt. Millions and millions of people have overcome their tobacco habit. There are as many former smokers in the population as there are current smokers. Willpower goes a long way, as does adequate preparation and support. I suggest you communicate the following message to smokers who want to quit: *"It's hard. It can be done. You can do it."*

For a good beginning, you can suggest they write down their reasons for quitting, establish their quit date, and write a "Goodbye Letter" to tobacco (see p. 146).

Reasons for Quitting

I recommend that people who plan to quit smoking write a list of their reasons, or if they prefer, an essay on the subject. Then I suggest they keep this list or essay nearby at all times to remind themselves of their position. A comprehensive list includes bad things that they will avoid (cough, disease, bad breath, being a slave to a drug, etc.) and good things that will happen as a result of quitting (breathing more easily, being better able to run, their food tasting better, etc.). Quitters should review the list periodically and every time they are tempted to use tobacco.

Quit Date

One of the best ways of moving from thinking about quitting to taking action is by setting a quit date. It could be after completing a program of gradually reducing the amount of tobacco smoked, or after breaking the pattern of smoking (see previous chapter). Sometimes people select quit dates that have special significance for them, such as New Year's Day or a birthday. Sometimes they pick a time when stress should be down, such as after a semester in school. But it is important to set a date.

Most smokers quit "cold turkey," which means abruptly, without first reducing the amount smoked. For smokers who prefer to gradually reduce, there are two different approaches. One is to reduce the number of cigarettes smoked each day. For example: Go from 20 to 18 to 16 to 14 cigarettes. Another approach, called postponing, is to delay the time at which the first cigarette is smoked, a little bit more each day. For example, the first day the first cigarette would be at 8 AM, the next day at 10 AM, the following day at noon. Regardless of the approach, I recommend spending no more than two weeks on the program. Longer periods of time could make quitting more difficult or become a form of procrastination.

A Goodbye Letter to Tobacco

Although not a requirement, writing a goodbye letter to tobacco can be a source of empowerment. It's an opportunity to express all the many feelings that go along with quitting. It has been said that there is a grieving process involved in giving up tobacco. To some people, it is like losing a dependable friend who has been a big part of their lives. The goodbye letter can help with the grieving process, allowing people to see the extent of their attachment to tobacco as well as their need for support.

What to Expect When You Quit

It's our hope that many teens will quit before they reach the point of addiction. However, addicted smokers who quit should be aware of the withdrawal symptoms they may experience. Other than intense craving, which is inevitable, there is much individual variation. Physical symptoms of nicotine withdrawal may include increased appetite, increased production of phlegm, cough, sweating, muscle aches and cramps, constipation or diarrhea, nausea, headache, sleep disturbance, and weight gain. Psychological symptoms may include irritability, restlessness, anxiety, depression, decreased tolerance for stress, and increased aggressiveness.

While being realistic about the withdrawal process, we also want to emphasize the positive side. The withdrawal symptoms pass their peak after two or three days, then drop off rapidly, reaching a substantially reduced level in about one week. As to cravings, willpower is a strong antidote. Furthermore, cravings come in waves. A person quitting has to try to ride these waves until they pass. After 30 to 90 seconds, the urges subside.

On an average, people gain five pounds when they quit smoking, which can be a significant concern to an adolescent. However, there are actions that can be taken to prevent weight gain. One of the most important ones is to start a program of physical activity. Other preventive measures recommended by the American Cancer Society in their brochure, *Smart Move! A Stop Smoking Guide*, include planning meals, eating less sugar, drinking extra water (six to eight glasses per day), substituting low-calorie snacks (raw vegetables, popcorn, etc.), and weighing oneself on a daily basis. Furthermore, research has shown that any weight gain that does occur is usually temporary and lost within 12 months.

One further problem associated with quitting is that *stress levels rise* in anticipation of the quit date, and actually peak before quitting. The reassuring news is that once the quit day finally arrives, anxiety begins to fall. Nevertheless, many smokers worry that when they quit, they are losing one of their tools for coping with stress. However, they should be informed of some surprising and encouraging research results: It has been found that overall perceived stress levels drop dramatically within a month of quitting. After six months, perceived levels are cut in half.

Tips for Quitting

To maximize success, people who are breaking a tobacco habit can benefit from a body of collective wisdom, some of which is described below.

Quit date: Set a quit date, and stick to it.

Tell people: Tell your family, friends, and other people you respect that you will be quitting. You even could try to recruit others to stop with you, so you would have their support.

Review previous efforts to quit: If there have been previous attempts, figure out what helped and should be repeated. Figure out what led to relapse, and how it can be avoided this time.

Start an exercise program: In his book, *The No-Nag, No-Guilt, Do-It-Your-Own-Way Guide to Quitting Smoking,* physician/author Tom Ferguson writes, "Exercise provides many of the same rewards as smoking—mental sharpening, an increased sense of control, and a greater ability to relax." This makes it an excellent way to prepare for, and support, your attempt to quit.

Start creating islands of peace: When you ask people about their motivation for smoking, they almost always speak of it as a way to deal with stress. People who want to quit smoking will have to find new ways to manage their stress. Psychologist and author Kenneth Pelletier, in his book *Mind as Healer, Mind as Slayer,* discusses the concept of islands of peace. He discovered that high-performing individuals tend to take time off for little "stress vacations" in the midst of very pressured and productive days. He called these interludes "islands of peace." They prevent stress from accumulating. Pelletier observed that "smoke breaks" not only provide the calming pharmacological effects of tobacco but also serve as an island of peace in which smokers temporarily put aside their everyday troubles. To compensate for losing this, people who want to quit smoking should think about establishing healthy new islands of peace in their lives. It could include taking time to relax with deep breathing, stretching exercises, or muscle relaxation. It could mean establishing regular "quiet times" to think. It could include regular aerobic exercise. Perhaps taking time to listen to relaxing music, or just to call a friend. Adolescence is a stressful time of life. Teens need these islands of peace as much as adults do.

The day you quit: Clean the environment. Throw away that last pack of cigarettes. Get rid of ashtrays in your home and everywhere you smoke. Toss the lighter into the trash. If you use smokeless tobacco, get rid of all tobacco products, spitting cups, and spitoons. Try to rid your personal environment of the smell of tobacco. Keep very busy all day. Try to stay away from smokers as much as you can, especially in the early stages of quitting. Begin drinking extra water, preferably six to eight glasses per day.

Focus on the benefits of quitting: Remind yourself of the benefits of what you're doing: You'll feel great about taking control of your life. Many positive physical changes will take place (see chapter seven, page 133). Review your own personal list of reasons for quitting.

Reward yourself: Save all the money you would have spent on tobacco products in a visible place, such as a glass jar, and then spend it on little rewards for yourself. Praise yourself all day long. For example, tell yourself: "I'm doing a great thing. I'm being strong. I'm taking care of my body. I'm taking control of my life."

Ride the waves: Episodes of craving tobacco come in waves lasting 30 to 90 seconds. First, realize that the urges to smoke will pass. They subside in a short period of time. Distracting yourself is a good tactic. You can take some deep breaths to calm down. You can chew gum, or go for a walk, or munch on a carrot. You can drink water. Psychologist Alan Marlatt teaches his patients to think of the craving as a wave and to watch it crest and fall. Also, keep in mind that how much and how often you crave will decrease as time passes.

Get social support: Ask for what you want from friends and family. For example, ask that they never offer you tobacco products. Perhaps you want to ask them to refrain from smoking in your presence. Ask for their encouragement. Identify and establish a support system for yourself: make arrangements to call nonsmoking friends or family members for support when you feel an urge to smoke. Identify a local hotline that you can call for help.

Prepare for mental tricks: Be prepared for the ways your "addictive voice" wants to get you smoking. Have your answers ready. For example:

Addictive Voice

Just one won't hurt.

Answer

It would definitely hurt. It would get me back on tobacco. I decided to quit. So I'm not going to take even take a single puff.

Addictive Voice

You're stressed out, you need a smoke.

Answer

Smoking will only help for a little while. It won't solve my problem. And then I'll have a bigger problem: I'll be smoking again. No way.

Learn the basic triggers: Some of the basic triggers for tobacco use include: being around other people who smoke; drinking alcohol; being under time pressure; feeling stressed; getting into an argument; celebrating; or feeling sad, anxious, bored, or frustrated. Be clever. For example, when tempted to smoke because of feeling bad, ask yourself, "Will smoking a cigarette solve this problem?" Be prepared: plan ahead for how you will deal with all your triggers.

Know at least the basics of mood management: Be prepared with knowledge of relaxation techniques (deep breathing, muscle relaxation) and ways you can distract yourself (taking a warm shower, exercising, drinking a glass of cold water). Chapters three and four can help you with this.

Find substitute activities for your mouth and hands: Many people find it helpful to have something available to put in their mouths ("mouth toys") or hold in their hands. Chewing gum, crunchy vegetables (such as carrot sticks and celery), fruit, toothpicks, sunflower seeds, or licorice are some ideas for the mouth. Many smokers have a whole ritual with their smoking. They tap their pack of cigarettes on a table. Pull out a cigarette. Tap the cigarette. Pull out the lighter. Hold it. Light the cigarette, and then hold the cigarette in their own unique way. You can replace this ritual with something different, a substitute activity for your hands, such as playing with koosh balls, stress balls, or hand exercisers.

Clean your mouth: Brush your teeth often and admire how clean they look. For people who have dipped or chewed smokeless tobacco, it is recommended in the American Cancer Society brochure, *Quitting Spitting,* that you get your teeth professionally cleaned soon after quitting. Smokers can do this as well.

Keep busy: Boredom is sometimes hard for ex-smokers. Find activities to keep your mind off tobacco.

Consider counseling and the use of nicotine replacement therapy: Individual or group counseling increases the success rate of smoking cessation. The longer the duration of the counseling and the greater intensity of the help, the greater the impact. Nicotine replacement therapy, through either the nicotine patch, nicotine gum, nasal sprays, or inhalers, also increases cessation rates and has been used with addicted adolescents. Counseling and nicotine replacement together help more than either alone. Nicotine replacement is of no value if used incorrectly. It is best to consult with a physician if you use this approach.

Develop a Personal Plan for Success

The most comprehensive way to prepare for quitting is by making individualized plans. Smokers identify their own unique high-risk situations—or "triggers"—for tobacco use. Then they devise ways to counteract these triggers. Clinically, this is known as "relapse prevention." I've noticed that young people dislike the negative connotation of preventing something bad from happening. Therefore, when talking with teens, I prefer to call this process "planning for success."

The theory is that we can anticipate triggers, prepare for them, and prevent relapses. An analogy can be made to conducting fire-safety inspections and fire drills. Inspections are to prevent fires. Drills are to prepare for them—to minimize harm—should the need arise. You wouldn't want to wait until after a fire is raging to hold safety inspections or to conduct drills. By the same token, you shouldn't wait until the triggers and urges to smoke have occurred to figure out how to counteract them.

Planning for success begins with smokers' gaining full awareness of their patterns of use. They can review past experiences to start identifying their triggers, or chart their smoking habits as described in chapter seven, under the heading "Recognizing the Patterns and Breaking Them."

I suggest that smokers classify and write down triggers for tobacco use in each of the following categories:

- Emotions
- People
- Situations or events
- Places
- Thoughts

Then smokers can begin planning for success by asking themselves these questions:

- Which of these triggers can I avoid? How can they be avoided?
- When triggers are unavoidable, how will I cope with them? That is, how will I cope with each emotion that triggers tobacco use? Each situation? Each person? Each event? Each place? Each thought?

Ideally the answers to these questions should be written down, in a document that becomes the Plan for Success. Here is an example of one person's planning for success. Sixteen-year-old David was a bright boy who had been smoking for two years, was addicted to tobacco, and smoked almost a pack a day when he decided to quit. With the help of his parents, and the backing of a psychologist, he came up with these ideas, all of which he eventually implemented.

- David admitted that he used to sneak a cigarette first thing every morning. When he quit, he started a ritual of going straight to the shower as soon as he woke up. The shower relaxed him and made it easier to cope with his urge to smoke.

- David realized that most of his smoking was with certain friends. He called each one to tell them he was quitting, to ask them not to smoke around him, if possible, and to ask that they never again offer him a cigarette.

- David knew it would be hard not to smoke when he was with a group of his friends, saw them lighting up, smelled the smoke, and wanted to be part of the scene. He decided to avoid being with his friends for a couple of days after he quit. He arranged to spend most of his time at home or with his girlfriend, who did not smoke.

- David knew that eventually he would be with his friends who smoked. He decided he would tough it out when they lit up. If he got tempted, he would leave for a short while to get away from the temptation. If friends offered him a cigarette, he would politely refuse it. He would also remind them that he has quit smoking, and ask that they stop making the offers.

- David realized that he smoked when he was feeling tense or stressed out. He decided he would do a physical workout whenever he felt stressed and had available time. If that wasn't possible at that moment, he had a whole menu of other coping options, such as listening to music, deep breathing and watching television.

- Much of David's stress involved problems with his parents, especially the ones related to how late he stayed out and where he was spending time. He asked his parents to be "easy" on him for a while. He also decided to stay mostly at home for a few weeks, simply to avoid hassles with his parents.

- David realized that he always carried his lighter with him. It was part of his smoking ritual. With reluctance, he decided to throw it away. He started carrying Lifesavers and other types of hard candy in his pockets.

- David knew how he might trick himself into smoking: "You've had a tough day. You deserve a cigarette." He prepared his answer for that thought. "Yes, it's been a tough day, but I'm proud of myself for quitting smoking. I absolutely do not want a cigarette. It would totally ruin my day."

As you can see, much of what occurs when people quit tobacco can be anticipated.

Despite the best-laid plans, urges to smoke may feel overwhelming at times. For this reason, it is wise to address the questions: What if all else fails? What will I do if my plan isn't working and my determination to quit is seriously wavering?

David made a backup plan for handling "emergencies." He decided he would call certain key people (his parents, his psychologist, or his girlfriend) for support if he was seriously tempted to smoke. He carried their phone numbers in his wallet. If he was tempted while visiting his friends, he decided that he would leave the scene fast. If he still felt the urge to smoke, he would put on his Walkman and go jogging, even at night. By the way, David successfully quit on his first attempt and remains tobacco-free to this day, now more than two years later.

Role Playing

Role playing is a great way to fortify a person's determination to quit using tobacco. David, discussed in the previous section, benefited from an opportunity to role-play various situations. His psychologist played the role of his best friend. In this role, he offered David cigarettes. David practiced different ways of refusing the offer. Another good situation is to have someone role-play an addictive voice that says: "You know you want to smoke. Go ahead. It'll feel good." The person quitting needs practice in standing up to that voice.

Lapse vs. Relapse

The goal in quitting tobacco is that this drug will never, ever be used again. Many people succeed in quitting on their first attempt. We want to encourage young people to feel that they can be successful. On the other hand, we need to be realistic in noting that it usually takes more than one attempt to successfully overcome a tobacco addiction. Good planning increases the likelihood of success. But things don't always work out the first time. We can let quitters know that a single lapse—having one cigarette or a few cigarettes, or smoking one night—does not mean that the effort to quit should be abandoned. A *lapse* is not the same as a *relapse*, which means resuming the old levels of use. The ideal response to a lapse is to say, "Oops, I goofed. I better get back on track. I also want to learn from this goof so I don't repeat it." We can be supportive of people who lapse by saying: "You can do it. You can get back on track. Don't let one lapse defeat you." Even when people relapse completely, we should remain supportive: "You can learn from this experience and try again. Quitting takes practice."

Full Circle: A Tobacco-Free Lifestyle

Tobacco prevention and tobacco cessation are two sides of the same coin. They are both about empowering people to live healthy lives and to meet their needs without using a dangerous drug: tobacco. With prevention, we reduce the drug-neediness quotient so that smoking will not be seen as the best or only way to satisfy important personal needs. For some children, however, we are too late. They are already using tobacco. But our goal remains the same: healthy living without a drug. We want to empower smokers to meet their needs and have a good life without tobacco. That way, they are in a position to reject tobacco—to make the decision to quit. As they use their personal power to overcome their tobacco habit, they will feel good about themselves.

CHAPTER NINE

A Final Word to Parents

In our drug-filled society, polluted by tobacco advertisers who spend billions of dollars trying to persuade our children to use their products, it's not surprising that adolescents, and even younger children, experiment with tobacco. We wish they wouldn't even touch this very dangerous and highly addictive drug.

The tobacco industry has money, but we parents have love, respect, and intelligence on our side. This is a battle for the health of our children that individual families can, and must, win. We want our children to base their decisions about tobacco on what they learn in our homes, not on the seductive and misleading advertising of greedy corporations, nor on the legacy of "coolness" it has left behind.

The good news is that we can make powerful counter-moves to protect our children from tobacco addiction. In doing this, we also strengthen them as individuals, protect them from the abuse of other drugs, and strengthen our own families. With effective education and dialogue, we can inculcate anti-tobacco attitudes that vastly decrease the percentage of young people who try tobacco. We can redefine "cool" so that vulnerable adolescents, seeking social acceptance, will be less inclined to gravitate toward peers involved in unhealthy behaviors. We can reduce the lure of tobacco, or any other drugs, by teaching our children how to satisfy their social and emotional needs in healthy ways. We can create open family discussions in which our children talk with us about important health decisions.

Even when we are too late for prevention, there is much that can be done to help regular or addicted smokers. We can help them rethink their choices, and assist them as they move through the various stages of change, ultimately culminating with a decision to quit. When they to choose to be tobacco-free, we can assist and support them in breaking the habit.

One other good way to show our children that we mean business, and to stand up for our children's future, is by participating in community action against the tobacco industry. We can support prevention efforts that have been proven successful in changing attitudes about tobacco, and reducing its prevalence, such as raising taxes on tobacco products; counter-advertising with messages promoting negative images about tobacco; providing merchant education about adolescent tobacco use and the laws prohibiting tobacco sales to minors; enforcing tobacco laws; involving schools in various programs, including those that provide school-based curricula; establishing tobacco-free environment policies; and restricting the advertising and promotion of tobacco products.

The battle lines are clear. On one side is a toxic, addicted lifestyle and a retreat from reality. On the other side is a tobacco-free lifestyle in which individuals feel empowered to have fun, excitement, and pleasure in life; to cope with stress; to feel comfortable with peers and in other social situations; and to successfully manage their emotions. In this book we are not just talking about choosing to be tobacco-free. We are also talking about living healthy, happy, and satisfying lives, which is an attainable goal for our children.

▪ Resources ▪

There are many publications on overcoming tobacco addiction. Although these resources have been geared to adults, many of the same principles apply to adolescents.

Excellent free literature is available from the American Cancer Society. They can be reached at 1-800-227-2345 or www.cancer.org. The Agency for Health Care Policy and Research also has good publications, which can be accessed at phone number 1-800-358-9295 or www.ahcpr.gov.

On the topic of overcoming tobacco addiction, I recommend the following books:

David Antonuccio, *Butt Out: A Compassionate Guide to Helping Yourself Quit Smoking, with or without a Partner*. Saratoga, Calif.: R&E Publishers, 1993.

Tom Ferguson, *The No-Nag, No-Guilt, Do-It-Your-Own-Way Guide to Quitting Smoking*. New York: Ballantine Books, 1987.

Terry A. Rustin, *Quit and Stay Quit: A Personal Program to Stop Smoking*. Center City, Minn.: Hazeldon, 1994.

Robert Schwebel, *Saying No Is Not Enough: Helping Your Kids Make Wise Decisions about Alcohol, Tobacco, and Other Drugs—A Guide for Parents of Children Ages 3 through 19*. New York: Newmarket Press, 1998.

Julie Waltz, *No Ifs, Ands, or Butts: A Smoker's Guide to Kicking the Habit*. Tucson: Northwest Learning Associates, 1989.

◼ Acknowledgments ◼

I would like to thank some of the many people with whom I have worked recently on issues related to tobacco and other drugs. Marilyn Civer has been a good friend and a strong advocate for healthful living. Cindy Garcia, Wendy Pipentacos, Deborah Brook, Kathy Gordon, Jon McCaine, and Andres Guariguata have all been thoughtful colleagues who helped me think through a variety of health and tobacco issues. I have had supportive dialogue with Dr. Benjamin Spock and Mary Morgan. My old colleagues in the Bay Area still influence my work after many years apart. I especially thank Claude Steiner for what he taught me. Philip Cowan and Sam Baskin were also important in my education. I am always grateful to the people who give me an opportunity to work on developing my ideas and programs. So I thank Fletcher McCusker, Gina Murphy-Darling, and Pam Clark-Reines at Providence Corporation. I also thank my agent, Al Zuckerman, and Esther Margolis, president of Newmarket Press.

At Newmarket, I am appreciative of Keith Hollaman, who was a wise and supportive editor. I thank Theresa Burns for her careful editing of the manuscript and Elissa Altman, John Cook, and Dorothy Gribbin, who took over as editors at the end. I also want to mention Harry Burton, who provides much support.

I am most grateful to my wife, Claudia Schwebel, who always helps me think through my creative efforts and provides enormous support, and to my parents, who are sharp thinkers and good editors, even in their mid-eighties. My sons, Frank and Henry, teach me a great deal about children. My thanks, too, to Davy, Sara, and Carol Schwebel.

▪ Notes ▪

Foreword

ix . . . tobacco addiction is a pediatric disease   David A. Kessler, *Oral Remarks: The Samuel Rubin Program.* Columbia University School of Law, New York, March 8, 1995.

Chapter One

4 Eighty-nine percent . . . started before they turned eighteen Center for Substance Abuse Prevention, "Growing up Tobacco Free," *Prevention Pipeline* (January/February 1995): 38–41.

Also, early adolescence is the peak age . . . smokeless tobacco U.S. Department of Health and Human Services, *Preventing Tobacco Use Among Young People: A Report of the Surgeon General* (Washington, D.C.: U.S. Department of Health and Human Services, 1994).

5 Of the three thousand Americans . . . one of three . . . will die prematurely   *Ibid.*

8 However, there are also considerable knowledge gaps   Donald W. Hine, Craig Summers, Kate Tilleczek, and John Lewko, "Expectancies and Mental Models as Determinants of Adolescents' Smoking Decisions," *Journal of Social Issues* 53, no. 1(1997): 35–52.

8-9 Researchers found that 73 percent . . . were still smoking after five years   Michael J. Meyers, "Saving the Children," *Professional Counselor* (December 1996): 43.

9 A recent study found that . . . teenagers will end up smoking . . .   Center for Substance Abuse Prevention, "A Giant Leap Forward in Tobacco Control," *Prevention Pipeline* (March/April 1997): 4–6.

11 Research studies have identified five stages of smoking initiation   B. R. Flay, "Youth Tobacco Use: Risks, Patterns and Control," in *Nicotine Addiction: Principles and Management*, eds. J. Slade and C. T. Orleans (New York: Oxford University Press, 1993).

15 . . . the enormous amount of caffeine consumed   Helen Cordes, "Generation Wired: Caffeine Is the New Drug of Choice for Our Kids," *The Nation*, 27 April 1998, 11–16.

Notes

Chapter Two

20 **Although the tobacco industry makes more than $270 million** John Slade, *Facts on Nicotine and Tobacco*, New Jersey Alcohol/Drug Resource Center and Clearinghouse, Clearinghouse Fact Sheet, Center for Alcohol Studies, Rutgers University, Piscataway, N.J., 1992.

... half ... own clothing or gear with cigarette logos David Pines, "Media Influence Is the Public Health Concern," *Prevention Pipeline*, Center for Substance Abuse Prevention (July/August 1996).

26 **... children and adolescents think that the prevalence of smoking is two or three times higher ... more likely to become smokers** U.S. Department of Health and Human Services, *Preventing Tobacco Use Among Young People: A Report of the Surgeon General* (Washington, D.C.: U.S. Department of Health and Human Services, 1994).

27 **Popular music, television ... portray various images** "Smoking, Drinking Are Prevalent on MTV," *The Arizona Daily Star*, 11 September 1997.

28 **... conversations to introduce ... pollution** Timothy A. Gerne and Patricia J. Gerne, *Substance Abuse Prevention Activities for Elementary Children* (Englewood Cliffs, N.J.: Prentice Hall, 1986).

Chapter Three

47 **You want to make sure that your children are emotionally literate** Claude Steiner, *Achieving Emotional Literacy: A Personal Program to Increase Your Emotional Intelligence* (New York: Avon Books, 1997).

47 **Studies have shown that children with lower self images ... more likely ... to use tobacco** U.S. Department of Health and Human Services, *Preventing Tobacco Use Among Young People: A Report of the Surgeon General* (Washington, D.C.: U.S. Department of Health and Human Services, 1994).

51 **The most successful drug prevention programs ... incorporate ... "alternative activities"** Maria G. Carmoona and Kathryn Stewart, "The Alternatives Approach: What Is It? Is It Any Good?" *Prevention Pipeline* (May/June 1996): 1–4.

166

56   **There is substantial research evidence about the benefits ...**
to reducing stress   K. L. Lichstein, *Clinical Relaxation Strategies*
(New York: John Wiley and Sons, 1988).

58   **The counterpart to relaxing muscles is breathing deeply**
Anne Kent Rush, *Getting Clear: Body Work for Women* (New York:
Random House, 1973).

67   **There is much research indicating that high expectations**
... foster high performance   Edward P. Sarafino, *Health Psychology: Biopsychosocial Interactions* (New York: John Wiley and Sons,
1994).

Chapter Four

72   **Those who report that tobacco serves "positive functions"**
... are at increased risk   K. E. Bauman, L. A. Fisher, E. S.
Bryan, and R. L. Chensworth, "Antecedents, Subjective Expected
Utility, and Behavior: A Panel Study of Adolescent Cigarette
Smoking," *Journal of Applied Social Psychology* 15, no.7 (1985):
606–621.

72   **Furthermore, a recent study showed that 78 percent ... pre-**
fer to date a nonsmoker   American Academy of Pediatrics,
Smoking Talk for Teens (Elk Grove Village, Ill., 1990).

82   **You should teach your kids assertiveness skills**   J. David
Hawkins, Richard F. Catalano, and Kathleen Burgoyne, "Parents as
Consultants and Educators on Peer Pressure," in *Parent Training Is
Prevention: Preventing Alcohol and Other Drug Problems Among Youth
in the Family*. Office for Substance Abuse Prevention, U.S. Department of Health and Human Services, Publication No. (ADM) 91-
1715 (1991).

83   **Coach them on loudness of voice**   Susan G. Forman, *Coping
Skills Interventions for Children and Adolescents* (San Francisco:
Jossey-Bass Publishers, 1993).

85   **... clear family position against the use of tobacco ... helps**
support a child   R. F. Catalano, E. O. Brown, P. F. Vadasy, C.
Roberts, D. Fitzmahan, N. Starkman, and M. Ransdell, *Preparing
for the Drug (Free) Years: A Family Activity Book* (Seattle: Comprehensive Health Education Foundation, 1988).

85   **. . . resistance skills are most helpful when . . . reviewed and practiced**   J. D. Hawkins et al., *op. cit.*

  . . . guidelines . . . helping your children say no . . .   *Ibid.*

Chapter Five

91   **. . . adolescents . . . need . . . more freedom, not less**   Jacqueline Eccles, C. Midgley, A. Wigfield, C. M. Buchanan, D. Reuman, C. Flanagan, and D. MacIver, "Development during Adolescence," *American Psychologist* 48, no. 2 (1993): 90–101.

101   **Roll with the resistance**   William R. Miller and Stephen Rollnick, *Motivational Interviewing: Preparing People to Change Addictive Behavior* (New York: Guilford Press, 1991).

102   **The stages of tobacco use**   B. R. Flay, "Youth Tobacco Use: Risks, Patterns, and Control," in *Nicotine Addiction Principles and Management,* eds. J. Slade and C.T. Orleans (New York: Oxford University Press, 1993).

104   **. . . experimentation . . . response to particular situations . . . or to a particular person**   R. A. Stern, J. O. Prochaska, W. F. Velicer, and J. P. Elder, "Stages of Adolescent Cigarette Smoking Acquisition: Measurement and Sample Profiles," *Addictive Behavior* 12, no.4 (1987): 319-329.

Chapter Six

117   **"young people should be made aware of the highly addictive nature of nicotine . . ."**   U.S. Department of Health and Human Services, *Preventing Tobacco Use Among Young People: A Report of the Surgeon General* (Washington, D.C.: U.S. Department of Health and Human Services, 1994), 71.

  . . . researchers asked high school seniors . . . if they thought they would still be smoking   L. D. Johnston, P. M. O'Malley, and J. G. Bachman, *Smoking, Drinking, and Illicit Drug Use Among American Secondary School Students, College Students, and Young Adults, 1975-1992,* Vol. II: *College Students and Young Adults.* U.S. Department of Health and Human Services, Public Health Service, NIH Publication No. 93-3481. Bethesda, Md. (1992).

119 **"foolish freedom"**   James O. Prochaska, John C. Norcross, and Carlo DiClemente, *Changing for Good* (New York: William Morrow and Company, 1994).

122 **. . . periods of unusually high stress . . . not the best times to quit**   Tom Ferguson, *The No-Nag, No Guilt, Do-It-Your-Own-Way Guide to Quitting Smoking* (New York: Ballantine Books, 1987).

123 **thinking pattern known as "cut-off"**   G. D. Walters, "Drug-Seeking Behavior: Disease or Lifestyle?" *Professional Psychology* 23, no. 2 (1992): 139-145.

Chapter Seven

133 **not-ready-to-quit smokers**   James O. Prochaska, Carlo DiClemente, and J. C. Norcross, "In Search of How People Change," *American Psychologist* 47 (1992): 1102–1114.

the benefits of quitting   American Cancer Society, *Smart Move: A Stop Smoking Guide* (1988).

Chapter Eight

141 **Tobacco . . . the most difficult addiction to break**   Andrew Weil, *Natural Health, Natural Medicine* (Boston: Houghton-Mifflin, 1990).

teens . . . experience relapse rates . . . similar to . . . adults   U.S. Department of Health and Human Services, *Preventing Tobacco Use Among Young People: A Report of the Surgeon General* (Washington, D.C.: U.S. Department of Health and Human Services, 1994).

142 **. . . we skip the important stages . . . that always precede action**   James O. Prochaska, Carlo Di Clemente, and J. C. Norcross, "In Search of How People Change," *American Psychologist* 47 (1992): 1102–1114.

146 **Symptoms of nicotine withdrawal**   Tom Ferguson, *The No-Nag, No Guilt, Do-It-Your-Own-Way Guide to Quitting Smoking* (New York: Ballantine Books, 1987).

The withdrawal symptoms pass their peak . . . then drop off rapidly   *Ibid.*

147 **Weight gain . . . is usually temporary**   Myra Muramoto, "Behavioral Approaches to Smoking Cessation," in *Difficult Choices* (Phoenix: Maricopa Integrated Health System, 1998).

 stress levels rise in anticipation of the quit date . . . drop dramatically within a month of quitting   David Antonuccio, *Butt Out: A Compassionate Guide to Helping Yourself Quit Smoking, with or without a Partner* (Saratoga, Calif.: R&E Publishers, 1993).

150 **. . . think of the craving as a wave**   Rebecca A. Clay, "Meditation Is Becoming More Mainstream," *American Psychological Association Monitor* 28, no. 9 (September 1997):12.

152 **Counseling and nicotine replacement together**   M.C. Fiore, W. C. Bailey, S .J. Cohen, et al., *Smoking Cessation: Information for Specialists, Clinical Practice Guidelines. Quick Reference Guide for Smoking Specialists, No. 18*. U.S. Department of Health and Human Services, Public Health Service, AHCPR Publication No. 96-0694, Rockville, MD (April, 1996).

Chapter Nine

159 **. . . prevention efforts that have been proven successful** Substance Abuse and Mental Health Services Administration, *Reducing Tobacco Use Among Youth: Community-Based Approaches*, Publication No. (SMA) 97-3146 (Washington, D.C.: U.S. Department of Health and Human Services, 1997).

❊ Index ❊

A

Achieving Emotional Literacy
(Claude Steiner), 59
activism
community, against tobacco industry, 159
consumer, and pollution, 28
activities
after-school, paying attention to,
51
alternative, to drug use and
crime, 51
art, in fighting tobacco use, 26
addiction
discussing with children, 115-
117
good health practices and prevention of, 14-17
meaning of, 107
of parents, 24
risk of, 8
stopping progression toward, 13-
14
to tobacco
as toughest to break, 24, 34, 141
as pediatric disease, ix
adolescents. *See also* teens; responses
ambivalence of, in getting
parental help, 143
effectively influencing behavior
of, 93-94
engaging in dialogue with, 42
factors influencing future use of
tobacco, 44-45

number who smoke, 2
and personal limits, 132
and smokeless tobacco, 4
in a time of exploration, 100
advertising and promotions of tobacco industry
aimed at children, 4-5, 21-23
community action against, 159
examples of, 4-5, 20, 26
teaching children to be suspicious of, 25-27
as threat to public health, 22
Agency for Health Care Policy and
Research, 161
American Academy of Pediatrics,
31, 38
American Cancer Society, 35-36,
147, 151, 161
American Heart Association, 35
American Journal of Public Health,
27
American Lung Association, 36
anger, as contributor to smoking,
47
art activities, use of in fighting tobacco industry, 26
assertiveness, 78, 79, 84
and aggression, distinction between, 81
reasons people avoid, 79
role playing, 82-84
attitudes
anti-tobacco, 35-36, 38, 158
consumer, and health education,
15-16

entertainment. *See* television
environment
  hazards in, 16-17
  stimulating, providing a, 67
  toxins in, 16
exchange-of-information model,
  92-97, 139
  final phase of, 126-127
  use in responding to rationaliza-
    tions, 114
exercises
  aerobic, 149
  deep-breathing, 58-59, 134, 148
  and physical fitness, 17, 148
  stretching, 148
experimentation, with tobacco,
  prevention of, 41

F

family meetings, 61
feelings. *See* emotions; moods;
    stress
Ferguson, Tom, 6, 148
friendship, teaching children
    about, 75
frustration and failure, as contrib-
    utors to smoking, 47

G

goals, helping children set, 67
guidelines, key, to help children
    say no, 85
gum disease, caused by tobacco,
    35, 38

H

"hanging out," 51
health education, and consumer
    attitudes, 15-16

health practices, good, use of in
    preventing tobacco addiction,
    14-17
heart disease, smoking and, 38
high-risk situations, avoiding, 87-88
home, climate of, 42-43, 60, 95
household substances and environ-
    mental hazards, 16-17

I

I statements, 63-64
inhalers, as nicotine replacement
    therapy, 152
intervention, at different stages of
    tobacco use, 102-107
islands of peace, 148-149

J

Journal of Pediatrics, 15

L

lapse vs. relapse, 156
laryngitis, caused by tobacco, 34
leadership skills, helping children
    develop, 76-77
lifestyle
  changes in, 135
  tobacco-free, 157
listening, 97. *See also* dialogue
lung cancer, and cigars, 38

M

Marlatt, Alan, 150
mastery approach to living
  assessment of, 65-70
  discussions of, 70
  to living, 65
  to school work, 69-70

media literacy, 25
medicines, use of in family, 16
Mind as Healer, Mind as Slayer
    (Kenneth Pelletier), 148
mistakes, handling, 68
Monitoring the Future Project
    (University of Michigan), 2-3
mood management, basics of, 151.
    See also emotions; stress
muscle relaxation, 148

N

nasal sprays, as nicotine replace-
    ment therapy, 152
nicotine, 12, 34
    dependence and addiction, 12-13
    gum, 152
    patch, 152
    physiological need for, 12
    replacement therapy, 152
    withdrawal, symptoms of, 146
*No Ifs, Ands, or Butts: A Smoker's
    Guide to Kicking the Habit*
    (Julie Waltz), 114
*No-Nag (The), No-Guilt, Do-It-
    Yourself Guide to Quitting
    Smoking* (Tom Ferguson), 6,
    148
no, ways to say, 84-87

P

pancreatic cancer, and tobacco, 38
parenting, visionary, 42-43
parents
    approachability of, 66-67
    and teaching good nutrition, 15
    as helpers in quitting tobacco,
        143-144
    presenting their point of view,
        95-96

as problem-solving partners, 68-
    69, 94
response of, as factor of future
    tobacco use, 42-43, 45
who smoke, 23-24
patterns of tobacco consumption,
    recognizing and breaking,
    135-137
peer influence, 36, 79-81
    as factor in future tobacco use,
        45
    indirect/subtle, 120-121
    positive, 89-90
    for teens, 119-120
peer pressure. *See* peer influence
peer support, positive, 89-90
Pelletier, Kenneth, 148
perseverance, importance of in
    mastery approach of living, 67
pipe smoking, 38. *See also* smok-
    ing; tobacco
pollution
    concept of, 28
    kinds of, 28
    of one's body, 29
    of public places, 28
popular culture
    influence of, 27-28
    as minimizer of danger, 27-28
power plays, 81
Power Rangers, 77
powdered snuff. *See* smokeless
    tobacco
*Preventing Tobacco Use Among
    Young People* (Surgeon Gen-
    eral's Report), 2, 71
prevention efforts, support of,
    159
progressive relaxation, teaching of,
    56-58
punishment, as impediment to di-
    alogue, 94